About the author

The author is a Spiritualist, a spirit healer and a spirit writer. His work is used by funeral websites and religious organisations around the world. At any one time there are some sixty or seventy funeral or religious websites using his poems online (The Poems of Richard John Scarr). In one instance, one of his poems, *No Debt to Pay*, is engraved on the rear of the memorial stone of a young Canadian soldier who was killed in action in Afghanistan in 2008.

AT SUMMER'S END

RICHARD JOHN SCARR

AT SUMMER'S END

Vanguard Press

A CIP catalogue record for this title is
available from the British Library.

ISBN 978 1 80016 269 3

Vanguard Press is an imprint of
Pegasus Elliot MacKenzie Publishers Ltd.
www.pegasuspublishers.com

First Published in 2022

Vanguard Press
Sheraton House Castle Park
Cambridge England

Printed & Bound in Great Britain

Dedication

For Berry

AT SUMMER'S END

When our summer moves towards its close,
And season's change is nigh,
Bowing weary head to autumn's due,
To bid its last goodbye.

When seasons all have run their course,
Then all must wilt before.
The changing hue from green to gold,
And blossoms form no more.

But stay thy fears. For with ending years
Comes forth a brand-new dawn.
When gold reverts once more to green,
And young and new seasons born.

For thus awaits a brand-new spring,
Where youth and joy abide.
And life endures for ever more,
In the world beyond 'The Great Divide'.

1
PROLOGUE

I AM NOT DEATH. I AM TRANSITION.

IF YOU FEAR ME, IT IS SIMPLY BECAUSE YOU DO NOT UNDERSTAND ME. FOR IF YOU UNDERSTOOD ME, YOU WOULD KNOW I AM MERELY A DOORWAY THROUGH WHICH YOU MUST PASS ON YOUR JOURNEY HOME.

IF YOU SUFFER PAIN OR TRAUMA WHILE I AM DRAWING NEAR, IT IS NOT OF MY DOING. I WOULD NEVER HARM YOU. THAT IS NOT MY FUNCTION. GOD HAS ENTRUSTED ME WITH THE TASK OF SEEING YOU SAFELY FROM THIS LIFE AND INTO THE NEXT. THAT IS MY ONLY FUNCTION.

WHEN I COME TO YOU, IT IS OFTEN AS A FRIEND INTENT ON BRINGING YOU BLESSED RELIEF AS I SEE YOU SAFELY THROUGH THE VEIL. BUT ALWAYS GENTLE AND NEVER BEFORE THE TIME GOD HAS ALLOTTED TO YOU.

IF I SEPARATE YOU FROM YOUR LOVED ONES, IT IS ONLY TO REUNITE YOU WITH OTHERS IN THE HEREAFTER. BUT IT IS NOT

MY INTENTION TO KEEP YOU APART, AND I WILL EVENTUALLY BRING YOU ALL TOGETHER AGAIN IN THE LOVE AND LIGHT OF ETERNAL LIFE.

SO IF YOU CANNOT LOOK UPON ME KINDLY, PLEASE DO NOT FEAR ME. SIMPLY LOOK UPON ME AS A NECESSARY, BUT HARMLESS WAY HOME, TO WHERE AN IDYLLIC LIFE, AND ALL WHO WENT BEFORE, ARE WAITING TO WELCOME YOU.

Richard John Scarr

2
INTRODUCTION AND EXPLANATION

Hi there, fellow citizen of the Summer Land. If you do not recognise yourself, please read on, and then, hopefully, you will.

I think it is true to say that today, more than at any time in the past, that more people accept the fact that we have been on this Earth Plane many times before, and have lived many lives, albeit some of them probably very short indeed — perhaps even to the point of barely seeing the light of day. And although it is not my aim to preach to the converted, I do hope those who are just starting out on their spiritual pathway will be able to gain something from these ages. But my real aim is to reach out to those who have little or no knowledge of Spiritualism, or of how the other side functions — those who mistakenly believe that death is the end of all, and there is nothing more beyond. And I hope by the time they reach the end of these pages, they will come to appreciate that when William Shakespeare's Hamlet, Prince of Denmark said, "There are more things in Heaven and Earth, Horatio, than are dreamt of in your philosophy," they were indeed words of pure wisdom. All I am asking is that they keep an open mind as we proceed.

To even begin to comprehend Spiritualism, we must first understand that each and every one of us is in reality, two beings — a spirit being within a physical or human frame. The human side of us is created on the Earth Plane by our parents, and is destined never to leave it. In other words, it is a citizen of the Earth. But the spirit side of us was created on the other side of life, and in accord, it is a citizen of the Summer Land. Or, as it is also known, the Spirit World. And once our time on this plane comes to an end, the spirit side of us returns from whence it came, back to the Spirit World, because the spirit side, which is the real us, has always lived and always will live — simply because it is indestructible!

The human side of us is created for one purpose, and that is to play host to the spirit while it is on this plane.

3
THE SPIRIT IS WILLING

For the first few weeks after conception, it is little more than a developing human shell, until such time as the spirit enters. For the spirit is the source of life for the physical frame. Without the spirit, the human frame simply cannot live, and although the physical side of us is the host, the spirit side is the boss, so to speak. As such, it never ages beyond the prime of the human frame. This means literally that once the human side of us has reached its prime, then the spirit side stops ageing and only the human frame continues to do so.

The prime of a human being is usually somewhere between the age of twenty-one and thirty years. And from then on, provided nothing happens to prevent it, the frame will continue to act as the host until it is too old to go on, and simply wears out. But no matter how old the human side of us grows, we always feel young inside, because the spirit side of us remains young. Hence the saying, '*The spirit is willing, but the body is weak!*'

In the spirit world, we have complete and total freedom of choice. So, when we contemplate a return to the Earth Plane for yet another life span, we are shown in advance everything that lies before us on this side. All the joys, and all the pain and heartaches to come. Then it is left entirely up to us to decide whether to remain where we are or to make the journey to the Earth Plane. Should we decide to return, then we do so without any memory of what we were shown. We enter the foetus selected at a very early stage of the pregnancy. It is generally believed to be around the tenth week. Some suspect even earlier. But as you can see, whatever environment we are born into on this Earth, it is not really by accident of birth, since we knew in advance all that we were coming to, and we had elected to return.

This brings us to the point that while we might find some aspects of a future life attractive enough to encourage us to make the journey, when you consider the suffering some people have to endure, and in some cases just how short their life spans are, it makes you wonder why they ever consent to it in the first place. And yet, although they know in advance what they are coming to, and just how long or short their life spans are going to be, and what they are going to endure, they still elect to come. One has to conclude that in each and every case, they get exactly what they come for.

The reason I am drawn to this conclusion is because my own wife lost two children, a boy and a girl, neither of whom saw the light of day, and who have both grown up in Spirit. The very first time my son came through to me, he said, "I'm fine, Dad. But I had to come back because I still had a lot to do on this side. But I got what I came for!" What was it he got and took back with him? I honestly wish I could tell you! However, the implication of his words appears to be that he chose to leave the foetus and return to the Spirit World of his own volition, and as a result, the pregnancy was terminated.

We all have free will in the Spirit World. And if I have interpreted the message I received from my son correctly, then that free will appears to extend to being able to change one's mind about starting a new life here on Earth, even during the pregnancy and before the actual birth.

What does arise from this situation, however, is the fact that, although my wife carried them both for such a short time and neither saw the light of day, they did return to spirit as our son and daughter. I have been assured of this on two occasions. One of them very recently, that our son is the spitting image of me. And our daughter mirrors her mother.

It should be understood also, that when a child is born with a body or brain malfunction, it has nothing to do with the spirit, or the Spirit World. It was not ordained from the other side that the child should be born with mental or physical problems. The problem or problems, whatever they might be, stem from the earthly side of life, either as a result of a genetic fault

17

or something going wrong during the pregnancy. The spirit side was perfect when it entered the foetus and it will be again when it returns home to the Summer Land.

There is one point I would like to clarify before we go any further. I know the use of the word 'spirit', and 'Spirit World' conjures pictures in one's mind of a land filled with transparent and wisp-like people, but nothing is further from the truth. On the other side of life the inhabitants are as solid as we are on this. The reason it is called the 'Spirit World' is simply because we define our two beings as human and spirit, and it is the spirit that returns home. Hence the use of the name 'Spirit World'. But I can assure you the Spirit World has everything relevant to our wellbeing that this world contains, and a great deal more besides.

Now at the other end of the spectrum, when someone makes their transition back to the other side, we automatically say that they have died. But in reality, we could not die even if we wanted to! It is an impossibility! As I have already mentioned, we have always lived, and we always will. So, when the physical frame can no longer sustain the spirit being, through illness, accident or old age etc., then the spirit has no option other than to discard its human shell. At the point of permanent separation, and because it is the spirit that gives life to the physical being, the thing we call Death but which is, in reality, natural transition, then takes place. Meanwhile the spirit, with the help of a loved one or friend from the other side, returns from whence it came, back to the Summer Land. The human shell ceases to be a living being, and becomes a useless piece of lifeless flesh and bone. There is little that can be done with it other than to bury or burn it. But that is the only part of us that dies.

Yet, speak to a hundred people, and probably over two thirds of them will admit to a having a morbid fear of death, simply because they have no understanding of the Summer Land or how it functions. For if they did, they would know that death is something that will not, and cannot happen to them, and when the time comes for them to leave this Earth Plane behind, there will be nothing to fear but fear itself.

4
DON'T GRIEVE FOR ME

Don't grieve for me, I did not die,
I was merely called away.
I did not want to leave you,
Yet neither could I stay.

But I am just a thought away from you,
You need not speak a word.
Just think my name, and I will be near.
Every thought of yours is heard.

I know you cannot hear my voice,
Or see me when I am there.
But it is I who tilts that picture,
And moves the cushion on the chair.

I am that movement you're sure you see,
The butterfly kiss upon your hair.
The gossamer caress upon your cheek,
You touch, as you become aware.

Please try to smile, my dearest one,
Then I can smile with you.
For when you cry, it breaks my heart,
Then I am crying too.

So don't be sad I moved away,
I really did not travel far.
I still hear every word you say,
I am with you, no matter where you are.

Richard John Scarr

5
THE SPIRITUALIST RELIGION

Although Spiritualism is, for many, a religion in its own right, most Spiritualists hold other religious beliefs also. But whatever those other beliefs might be, Spiritualism is always at the forefront of those beliefs. By that I mean, irrespective of whatever god they might worship, in the final analysis they know that when they make their transition, they will return home to the Spirit World and into the bosom of all those family and friends who went before. For unlike some other religions, Spiritualism is not founded on the belief of something that happened centuries ago, or in the acceptance of a saviour yet to come. It is based on proof positive of life after so-called death! All around the world, and on a daily basis, mediums are providing evidence of life after death, and demonstrating that life goes on in the Spirit World.

"But do they really?" I hear you say.

Well, if a medium who has never met you before and does not know you from Adam tells you that your grandfather had a wooden leg, a glass eye and a tattoo of a snake on his backside; and also reminds you that as you were leaving home that day you accidentally trod on the cat's tail; and if your grandfather really did have a wooden leg and a glass eye — even if he never mentioned the tattoo — who but your grandfather could have passed that information on to the medium? And if you did tread on the cat's tail as you were leaving home, it proves your grandfather was actually there at the time and witnessed the incident.

Of course, there are other religions who also believe in life after death, but they simply do not know the wheres or the whys or how they and their loved ones make their transition. And for the most part, although they know that there is a place they go to once they leave the Earth, the mechanics are still something of a mystery to them. Because it is so, death still holds a fear for them. But Spiritualists, on the other hand, know exactly where their loved ones are, and how they made their transition. And so they know exactly how and where they themselves will eventually be going, and it holds no fear for them whatsoever. In fact, most Spiritualists look forward to their own transition to the Summer Land, and that includes me. For who would not look forward to making a transition to a world of love, light and tolerance, such as can only be imagined?

Spiritualists and Spiritualist mediums come from all walks of life, and from all cultures and creeds. I myself am a Christian Spiritualist, and believe in God the Creator. I can assure you there are Spiritualists from many other religions too, many of whom have the awareness and the ability to make a link with those living in the Spirit World. But not all Spiritualists are mediums. Millions of them simply believe and attend Spiritualist churches merely in the hope of receiving a message from their loved ones in the Spirit World.

So then, in view of the fact that Spiritualists do come from many backgrounds and hold various other religious beliefs, ideally, a Spiritualist church should be just that! A church where all Spiritualists, no matter what their faith might be, can attend without fear of having someone else's religion thrust down their throats.

For instance, when a Spiritualist of another religion attends a Christian Spiritualist Church in the hope of receiving a message from his or her loved ones in spirit, the last thing they want is a Christian hymn book thrust into their hand as they walk through the door, no more than a Christian would wish to be handed a prayer mat. And yet most Spiritualist churches, my own included, still cling to the Christian format, even though we claim we are open to all other religions, and we do hand out hymn books to everyone who enters without ever stopping to consider whether he or she is a Christian or of some other religious belief.

The ideal situation would be, of course, if all churches who are first and foremost Christian, were to state so in their advertising. But they should also make it clear that all Spiritualists, regardless of what their other religious beliefs might be, are also welcome. At the same time, they must not expect a non-Christian to pray in the Christian manner, or sing Christian hymns, and should therefore understand if someone of a different religion refuses the hymn book. And we Christians should always keep firmly in mind that when non-Christians come to our church, it is in order to receive messages from their loved ones on the other side, and not to be converted to Christianity.

So, being mindful and hopeful that people of all religious beliefs might be drawn to read these pages, when I write of God, I and other Christians think of him in the context of our own beliefs, while people of other faiths will of course think of him in the context of their own Almighty and their own religion. But in the final analysis, I have merely written these pages by telling it as I know it to be.

6
AND GOD SAID

Be not afraid, my precious ones,
When your time on Earth is through.
Death is but a change of life,
No harm will come to you.

No need to fret or worry,
When transition time is nigh.
Would I create my children,
Just to let them die?

For as your children are to you,
That is how you are to me.
And the tender love you feel for them,
I feel for you, my family.

You are all my sons and daughters,
Every colour, culture, creed.
And I placed you on the Earth, to love,
And to help each other's needs.

Although at times you may feel lonely,
We walk together, you and I.
I would never let you walk alone,
I am always at your side.

I share in all your pleasures,
Your heartaches and your pain.
As you learn the things that must be learned,
Whilst there upon the Earthly Plane.

No good deed goes unnoticed,
No kind gesture made in vain.
You will each receive your just rewards,
When I bring you safely home again.

Richard John Scarr

7
SAINTS AND SINNERS

Now although Spiritualists come from many races and many cultures, it is true to say Spiritualism is most popular in America, Canada, the UK, Australia and New Zealand. To a lesser extent, it is popular in some European countries also. And while some people are born with great awareness, others have to study and develop their awareness ability over a period of many years, by sitting in awareness groups, or circles as they are also known — and by attending Spiritualistic workshops etc. because it takes time, great dedication, aptitude and study in order to take to the platform before an audience as a competent medium. In fact, where Spiritualism is concerned, we never stop learning, or acquiring knowledge. But the ability is there in all of us to become a platform or healing medium. For we are, after all, a spirit in a human body, and it is the spirit side of us that does the spiritual linking with our loved ones on the other side.

So, then — when placed in its proper perspective, there is nothing very startling about a spirit on this side of life linking with a spirit in the Summer Land. On the contrary, it is in fact the most natural thing in the world, and with dedication and determination we can all utilise the spirit side of us to this end.

Mediums with the ability to link with those who have moved over to the Summer Land have always been with us. And today, especially with the help of television, Spiritualism has become very popular, thanks to mediums like Colin Fry (who has now made his transition to the Summer Land and will be greatly missed), Sally Morgan, Derek Acorah (also sadly no longer with us), Gordon Smith, Tony Stockwell, John Edward and Lisa Williams, to mention just a few. With the popularising of Spiritualism, most towns now have at least one Spiritualist church, or a venue where clairvoyance meetings are held.

A vast contrast, you might think, from the days when mediums were looked upon as witches, and subjected to the ducking stool or burned at the stake. And you would imagine then, the image of a witch stirring a cauldron and chanting, 'Leg of toad, wing of bat!' would be just a childish belief of days of old, and as such would be ridiculed by learned people. Especially learned modern-day people such as barristers, judges, government ministers, etc. But you would be wrong! Believe it or not, the 1735 Witchcraft Act was invoked as recently as 1944.

During the Second World War a woman named Helen Duncan was arrested and charged under this Act. She was placed in the dock at the Old Bailey, found guilty and sent to prison for nine months. It happened in the following way.

Helen Duncan lived in Portsmouth, and was reputed to be a clairvoyant, and as such she would hold séances. In 1941, while conducting one of these séances, she claimed to have linked with a sailor who had lost his life when, on the twenty-fifth of November of that year, the Royal Navy ship HMS Barham was torpedoed and sunk.

Now both the Admiralty and the War Office had in fact withheld the news of the sinking from the general public, and didn't announce it until January 1942. So as a result of her claim, she had come to the attention of the powers that be at that time. Then in 1944 she was arrested whilst conducting yet another of her séances, and she was charged with contravening the Witchcraft Act.

The authorities' case was that, although the news of the sinking of the Barham had been withheld from the general public in 1941, the next of kin of the sailors who had lost their lives had been informed at that time of the sinking. And they reminded the court that Duncan lived in the naval town of Portsmouth where things had a habit of coming to light. So, she could quite easily have heard of the sinking. They insisted that her claim to have received the information from a dead sailor was a false one. But to back her claim, Helen Duncan had produced a sailor's cap band, which she claimed had come into her possession by way of the link with the dead sailor, and it did indeed contain the name of the ship. But during the Second World War, British sailors had ceased to carry the name of their ship on their cap bands, and living in a naval town, Duncan would of course have known that. Yet she still insisted the cap band had been passed to her during the link with the sailor in question.

It should also be pointed out however, that over the years Duncan had been arrested several times and charged with fraud. It was also claimed that at various times she had produced what appeared to be ectoplasm from her mouth. It is alleged that on one such occasion, when someone present grabbed it, it was found to be cheesecloth. On another occasion it was said to be tissue paper treated with egg white. If true, then they were hardly the actions of a genuine medium. But whatever her alleged shortcomings, it does not alter the fact that invoking the ancient Witchcraft Act was absolutely outrageous.

It has been suggested that the real reason Duncan was arrested and sent to prison in 1944 was because the D-Day landings were pending. The authorities were afraid she might reveal information about it, and so alert the Germans. And if this was the case, then it would suggest they really believed her to be a genuine medium and capable of making the kind of links she claimed. But at the same time, it would also mean that those involved in putting her in the dock bent the law in order to get her safely tucked out of harm's way. And that certainly appears to be the case.

Prime Minister Winston Churchill is said to have been furious, called the case ludicrous and demanded to know why the ridiculous Act had been resurrected. He visited Duncan in jail, and promised he would do all he could to see it never happened again. As a result, in 1951, the 1735 Witchcraft Act was repealed, and it was replaced by the Fraudulent Mediums Act.

However, in spite of Churchill's determination to ensure it did not occur again, history repeated itself when, six months after Duncan was jailed, another woman, seventy-two-year-old Jane Rebecca Yorke, was also arrested and charged under the same Act. But this time, when the case was tried before a magistrate, although she was found guilty, the magistrate appears to have stuck two fingers up to those who tried the Duncan case. He appears to have demonstrated his feelings by not remanding Yorke for trial by a higher court but instead fining her just five pounds. Although a tidy sum in those days for a working-class person, it was nevertheless, a far cry from the sentence meted out to Duncan. The way Yorke was dealt with at her trial helped to highlight the miscarriage of justice to which Duncan had been subjected.

Did these two magistrates find themselves under pressure to convict? If so, then while the magistrate who tried Duncan remanded her for trial by a higher court, the magistrate who tried Yorke certainly turned the tables on those pressuring him. I believe even today Duncan's relatives are engaged in seeking a full pardon for her, which if refused would be just as ludicrous as the original charge. But either way, it would still be a case of the horse and the stable door.

Was Duncan a phoney? Or was she a genuine medium? Were the claims about the cheesecloth and the tissue paper true? Your guess is as good as mine. All I can tell you is that a great many people came forward to give evidence on her behalf, claiming they believed her to be a genuine medium, which of course means if the authorities were hell bent on locking her away (and it certainly looks that way) it was hardly the kind of evidence they would want to hear, and certainly would not have helped to get Duncan released.

The case left a bad taste in the mouth of British justice, and both the press and the public made it clear those responsible were being held up to ridicule. So much so, that even the judge attempted to bring a semblance of sanity back to the proceedings, by stating in his summing up that Spiritualism itself was not on trial. And neither he said, was he interested in whether manifestations were possible or not, which in the circumstances, was a strange thing to say. He went on to state that he had taken the jury's verdict of guilty to mean that they had found her guilty of dishonesty and fraud, even though the charge of fraud had been dropped and therefore was no longer relevant.

Although some seventy or more years have passed since the Duncan trial, and some facts might have gone through a change in the telling, what has not changed is the fact that those who were entrusted to uphold British justice did make a mockery of that justice by sinking to the level of delving into the realms of ancient folklore in their attempts to find the means by which to incarcerate Duncan for as long as was possible.

Today most, if not all of those involved with this travesty will now be on the other side, and I have little doubt they cringe with shame and embarrassment every time they cross Duncan's path.

But of course, there are charlatans in every business. For where there is money involved there is always going to be someone ready to chance their arm. And the world of clairvoyance is no exception. I myself encountered one such phoney, and it happened in the following way.

At the time of which I speak, I was the vice president of my Spiritualist church, and a woman was the president. She came to church one evening enthusing about a trance medium she had met, and was praising his abilities to the skies, although to my knowledge, she had not yet seen him work. So I assumed her enthusiasm was based on his, or somebody else's say-so.

A trance medium is one who goes into a trance, and the person with whom he or she is linking on the other side takes over the medium's body and speaks through them, while at the same time superimposing his or her own features over that of the medium's. This man was supposed to be such a medium. And so it was arranged he should give an evening of trance mediumship at our church.

Come the evening, things took a turn for the worse. First, he insisted the doors be locked. Why? I can only presume he wanted a captive audience. Then he insisted that a lamp be placed on the floor beside him with the light shining up onto the side of his face, and all the other lights switched off, which screamed 'Phoney'!

As children, one of the things we kids used to do was to hold a torch under our chins with the light shining upwards. In the dark this gives the face a very strange and eerie appearance, and when moving the head, it gives the impression one's face has changed. Even changing one's expression can produce a different look to one's features, and it was so obvious that this was the effect this man was aiming for. No genuine medium, trance or otherwise would have the lights switched off, or use the gimmick of a lamp shining up onto the side of his or her face. Neither of course, would they dream of insisting the doors be locked, in case of a fire.

The man started the evening by saying he would be taken over by a Russian, and then he began speaking in what he obviously considered to be a

Russian accent. I watched his face closely. But he was obviously not aware the lamp he was using was neither powerful enough, nor close enough to his face to have any effect on his features. No matter how much he moved his head, his features did not change. They remained his own face throughout.

Just how many of the audience were taken in by him, I don't know. But the president certainly was, and when the question of his genuineness was raised, it fell on deaf ears.

As the weeks went on, others began to voice their doubts also, but still to no avail. For the president still considered this phoney to be the best thing since sliced bread. Because some of us held a totally different opinion to hers as to the genuineness of the man's abilities, she took to arranging séances in her own home for her friends and relatives, rather than at the church, for which he no doubt demanded a fat fee.

But things got out of hand when the president took it upon herself to invite him on to the church committee without any referral to the rest of us. At that point I made up my mind to have absolutely nothing to do with any further events that he might be involved with. Finally, after various incidents which I won't go into, I decided I'd had enough and resigned from the church. However, less than a year later, I was to return again as its new president.

There came a time after I had left when the new vice president too began to smell a rat and suspect this man was not what he claimed to be. He engaged him in conversation and casually asked him if he had worked on the platform at any of the other local Spiritualist churches. The man reeled off the names of some of them where he purported to have worked. The vice president then phoned the presidents of these other churches to check the validity of the man's claims. Needless to say, not one president had even heard of him. And exactly as you might expect, when the phoney was called to task, he disappeared. To my knowledge, he has not been seen in the area since.

8
A CALM AND PEACEFUL JOURNEY

No need for fear, my darling,
When transition time is due.
When the moment comes to join me,
I will be there to bring you through.

It is a calm and peaceful journey,
Free from doubts and all alarms.
For you will travel gently through the veil,
Safely snuggled in my arms.

I will take you to the halls of rest,
Where you will wake up well again.
For in our World of Love and Light,
There is no suffering or pain.

I will be with you through your healing sleep,
To be the first one you will see.
And you will reach and gently touch my face,
To convince yourself it is really me.

Then all the loved ones you have lost,
And who have travelled on ahead.
Whom you thought you would never see again,
Will gather round your bed.

And when you are fully rested,
I will introduce you to our world.
And watch the wonder in your eyes,
As our Summer Land unfurls.

And when all your friends have gathered,
To add their welcome too,
I will take you home to the little house,
I have prepared for you.

Richard John Scarr

9
NOTHING SPOOKY

There is nothing spooky about Spiritualism, and certainly nothing to fear. We are not dealing with the paranormal, but with loved ones who have made their transition to the other side of life. The problem is of course, too many people still look on Spiritualism, and quite misguidedly so, as speaking to the dead! What utter nonsense! There is not a person on this Earth who can speak to the dead, well-known mediums included. And if this too sounds like a contradiction in terms, I assure you it is not.

The part of us that dies, is the human shell, and that is either buried to rot, or burned. And no one but no one can converse with that! What is dead is dead! But it is the only part of us that does die. The real us, the spirit us, and still very much alive, goes home to the Summer Land. So if you hear someone claiming they can speak to the dead, they are telling porkies! They might well have the ability to converse with those in the Spirit World, but any claims they might make about being able to speak to the dead are simply an attempt to gild the lily, purely for dramatic effect.

There are in fact one or two well-known mediums who actually make this exaggerated claim, and they do so of course with their tongue firmly planted in their cheek, purely to create that dramatic effect. They know there is no death, and yet they still go on uttering these absurdities without any thought to the harm they are doing to the Spiritualist cause.

Our loved ones on the other side are not only doing more or less all those things they did on this side, but a lot more to boot! Time and time again people from the other side confirm that they are still indulging in their favourite sports etc. But more than that, the chance to study for things they could only have dreamed of doing on this side of life are open to them also — opportunities that, on this side, are only open to people who have had a good schooling, and a university education.

There are of course millions of people even today, who never get the opportunity to go to university for various reasons. But in the Summer Land we are all of equal worth. It does not matter how high you climbed, or what lowly status you held while living your current life span. On the other side the same opportunities are open to all. There are great halls of learning, where knowledgeable people are ready to tutor you on practically every subject we have here, and many we do not. There are huge libraries to support these halls of learning, and so you can, if you wish, study any subject your heart desires. Or not. It is entirely up to you. We are back to free will.

Now I know for some people, the idea of another world containing all that we have in this one, and more, filled with living beings to boot, and yet invisible to us on this side, is very difficult to comprehend. So let us deal with that point before we go any further.

When people talk of the Summer Land, or Heaven, they usually refer to it as being above. I do so quite often myself, in my poems. But I am merely taking advantage of poetic licence. For the Spirit World is neither above nor below our world. It runs parallel. But the reason we are out of sight of each other is because the Earth Plane and that of the Spirit World exist within totally different dimensions. And in between those two dimensions is what has come to be known as 'The Veil' or 'The Great Divide'. Our loved ones on the other side have the ability to hear even our thoughts, as well as our voices, and of course they can cross from one dimension to the other at any time they choose. Nevertheless, they cannot see us or the contents of this world until they actually cross back through that veil. Yet they know only too well, having lived in and left this world behind, that out of sight of them is the Earth Plane, containing all that it does contain.

Understandably then, by the same token it works in reverse! We on this plane cannot see the Spirit

World, and it is only when we cross that veil that we too can see their world and all that it contains. This brings us to the point that if our loved ones are solid in the Summer Land, then why is it we cannot see them when they visit with us here? Well, that is a good question! And one I myself pondered on for a long time.

Some time ago I read a book in which the author ventured that our loved ones do not actually leave the Spirit World when visiting our side of life, but in fact remain there, and merely project a 3D image of themselves over to the Earth Plane. He stated that by the time that 3D image reaches its destination it has been reduced to a 2D image and therefore is invisible to the average person.

Now at the time of reading that particular book, I have to say I tended to disagree with this 3D image idea. My own beliefs at that time were that the solid body of our loved ones remained in the Spirit World and it was their spirit that made the visit to this side of life. But I was to learn later, through my wife, that both these theories were wrong.

When returning to the Spirit World to stay, they do take on a solid form, and if the physical body has aged beyond its prime, the spirit being will be a younger version of the person they were on this side. When visiting this side of life, it is done by projecting the astral body by means of thought to where they wish to be on the Earth Plane. However, the astral body is created for just the environment of the Spirit World, as the human body is created for that of the Earth Plane. So once the astral body leaves the dimensions of its own plane to cross the divide and into the dimensions of the Earth Plane, everything changes. Matter changes! As a result, they cannot be seen by the average person on this side. Even for a medium to see them, the psychic energy has to be strong enough, such as during a clairvoyance meeting, or an awareness group. It is the fact that they cannot be seen by the average person on this side that leads some people to believe our loved ones have no body on the other side either. I recently heard a medium online claim that our loved ones in spirit have no eyes or ears. Obviously this was something he had been taught when starting out, and he had retained that belief to this day.

The fact is, of course, once they leave the Earth's dimension and move once more into their own, everything changes again, and their astral body is back to normal.

But coming back to this business of talking to the dead — if I thought for one second the dead were linking with me, then I would be the first one out of the door! And I have no doubt if they could, our loved ones in the Spirit World would kick the backsides of those silly people on this side who slander them by claiming they are dead.

10
FOLLOW MY DIRECTIONS

I know you miss the ones you love,
But they did not travel far.
And if you will follow my directions,
I will explain just where they are.

First, interlock your fingers,
And now, imagine your right hand
Is the Earth upon which you live,
And the left, the Summer Land.

And where your fingers interlock,
Is the veil that lies between.
That is just how close the two planes are,
And yet to each other, remain unseen.

Because we live in different worlds.
And the dimensions are not the same.
When we cross to theirs, or they to ours,
We are crossing onto different planes.

And though the veil is termed: 'The Great Divide',
It is really just a door,
Through which we pass when going home,
Or when crossing back once more.

And although our loved ones hear each word
Or thought, that we send out to them,
They cannot see our Earthly Plane,
Until they cross back through the veil again.

And by that token too, the same applies,
And in reverse, it is the same.
We cannot see the Summer Land,
Or all that it contains.

But it is there in all its glory,
As our loved one would affirm.
With all this world contains, and more!
As each of us will learn.

Halls of rest, great halls of learning,
Where learned people teach.
Any craft or skill our heart desires,
Is there within our reach.

Not the best just for the privileged,
As with most things here on Earth.
For no matter what our status here,
In God's Summer Land, we are equal worth!

And we take with us our foibles,
And our sense of humour too.
And the mistakes we make whilst we are here,
Are there to be reviewed.

We will not be judged, or criticised,
That task is left to us.
To repent the harm we did to others,
And forgive all those who were unjust.

We came here at our own behest,
And to think we die, is wrong.
We have been here many times before
Then returned back home, to where we belong.

Richard John Scarr

11
TRANSITION

Each time we come to this Earth it is with an allotted time after which we will make our transition back to the Summer Land again. And with that allotted time in place, we do not leave one minute before. Nor do we stay one minute after that time. But in order to make that transition, we all of us must have a way by which to pass from this Earth Plane. I have been asked several times why it is that some pass over very gently and peacefully, some pass very quickly, as with a heart attack etc., while others suffer lingering agony before finally departing this life.

As I have already stressed, we will all have been here many times before we make our very final transition to the Summer Land. Each time we come here it is for the purpose of learning and experiencing new things, both good and bad. So it would do no good returning to the same kind of life, to do the same kind things, or have the same kind of experiences, and then leave the Earth Plane in exactly the same way as in a previous life.

During the course of these lifetimes, we all learn what it is to suffer hardships and live a life of want, and we all learn what it is like to make a painful and lingering transition. And equally, we all learn what it is to live a life of privilege and get the best of everything. In other words, we all get to live the lives we see other people living.

So, then, the man riding around in a Rolls Royce and living the life of luxury today might, in a previous life, have been a homeless pauper sleeping rough, or earning a living that barely kept his head above water. You might have been a leper in India, or perhaps a member of the aristocracy, never knowing a day of want, and being waited on hand and foot. What is certain is the fact that when we have been here so many times, and have learned all there is to learn about being a spirit within a human shell — when we have been there, done it and got the T-shirt — then we too will make a gentle and peaceful final transition. And so, for most Spiritualists, it is not the going that gives any concern, but the way in which they go, each hoping they have already done the lingering, painful passing in a previous life.

What counts on the other side is the way we behaved on this, and how we handle both the hardships and the privileges of those lives we live on the Earth Plane. If we were on our uppers, and yet willing to give the shirt off our backs to someone even worse off than ourselves; if no matter how bad things were for ourselves, we were always ready to help those worse off, always ready to donate our time to the welfare of others; if we did our best to live a decent life, mistakes excepted; then we will certainly reap the rewards for that on the other side.

The same too goes for when we were living the good life on this side. If we were generous and did our best to help the less fortunate, then again, we will reap the benefits of those kindly acts. But equally, if we lived for ourselves alone, a life of selfishness; or if we were hard taskmasters and cruel to those who were dependent on us; or simply indifferent to the suffering of those around us when we could have helped; then we will reap what we have sown.

But I honestly believe, the more privilege we have, the more distant we grow from reality, and that is why we all experience privilege in at least one lifetime, because it is certainly a bigger test than that of being born poor.

For instance, if someone was in trouble, a person from the poorer classes will offer their services in any way they can. If a neighbour was sick and unable to get the kids their breakfast and get them off to school, someone in the street would step in and do what was necessary, including picking the kids up again after school. And they will also go round during the day to see the mother and see that she is OK, taking her broth or whatever.

Now, honestly, can you see Countess Wotsit visiting someone's working class home to do the same thing? She might, if she did not think it below her, send her chauffeur round with broth. But she certainly won't go round in person to get the kids their cornflakes, and make them a sandwich to take to school with them. The truth is of course, the privileged classes have little or nothing to do with poorer class people, so they probably don't know any, outside those who work for them. So it is true to say, the more privilege we have, the more we distance ourselves from the real world, and from the people outside that of which we consider to be 'our class'.

The real world of course, is one of survival. Of working to support our families and for everything we have. But the majority of the privileged are simply born into it. Some have their feet firmly planted on the ground, and appreciate that the luxury and the good life they are enjoying was simply down to the fact that it was there waiting for them when they were born. They are usually appreciative and good natured, and kindly to those less fortunate than themselves.

Unfortunately, there are some among the aristocracy and well off etc. who believe they richly deserve to be where they are, because they regard themselves as special. The elite! These are usually the plum-in-the-mouth type, whose whole life has been one of great privilege, and the best that money can buy. Public school educations, the finest universities and a guaranteed and privileged position in anything that is going. But the fact that they haven't lifted a finger to either earn or deserve it seems to elude them.

We have all met them of course. The kind who either just ignore the poorer classes as though they don't exist — or if they have to have any dealings with them, talk down to them and behave as though they are dealing with something the dog left on the pavement. Or, if they know your surname, they will address you by it, while deliberately omitting the Mister, just so you are in no doubt as to their superiority. So the test of humility, and all that goes with it is a lot harder for them than it is for the working or poorer classes. For the poorer classes are born to humility and little else.

However, if this kind of snooty person tends to rub you up the wrong way, try to remember they too came from the other side, and they are merely living an experience which, like yours, will be one of many before they make their final transition. And they are simply not handling the experience very well.

It might be as well to remember, if you haven't been already, then you too, during at least one lifetime, will be in their place, and living the life of the privileged. They too will get to experience yours, even though it is hard to imagine, say, a member of a royal family stacking shelves in a supermarket, or working as a school dinner lady, which they might very well have to do, or have already done in a previous life. It is hard too, to imagine President Wotshisname, or the Right Honourable Gumboil following behind a dustcart emptying dustbins — and yet the one thing we can be absolutely certain of, is no matter what our position or status is in the life we are living now, the next one will be totally different. What we should be asking ourselves is, when in the shoes of the privileged upper classes, how did we, or how will we behave? Grounded, and with kindness and humility towards others, and grateful for what we have accomplished? Or, as toffee-nosed idiots who have managed to convince ourselves we really are superior beings?

Jesus knew what a corrupting influence wealth could be for some people, and it was this kind of person he was referring to when he said, 'It is easier for a camel to pass through the eye of a needle than it is for a rich man to enter the Kingdom of Heaven.'

It is not difficult to understand then, just how much easier it is for someone leaving a poorer class life to make their transition to the other side, than it is for someone who has lived a life of the wealthy. For someone who has known nothing but privilege and great importance, it comes as a huge shock when they find they have no rank or special status in the Summer Land, but are now just one of the ordinary people, and are treated as such.

12
THE ROAD OF LIFE

Come with me. And let me be
Your guide, and let us take
A trip along the Road of Life,
We spirits choose to make.

Our start point is the Summer Land.
When we choose again, by birth,
To return for yet another life,
On the plane we call, The Earth.

And we are shown before we make each trip,
All we will suffer, lose or gain.
And we know too, when this life is through,
We will return from whence we came.

And so, once more upon this plane,
A spirit, in a human frame
Is born to learn what must be learned,
Then take that knowledge home again.

And though for some of us, our lives will be
Privilege-filled, and trouble-free,
Some will find no peace of mind,
And will live lives of a different kind.

Why then should this contrast be?
Why this gap, twixt thee and me?
Why should some be born to gain?
Whilst other suffer want and pain?

That question can be laid to rest,
For we knew before we made this quest.
That no matter if we rule, or serve,
Each life, is just a learning curve.

And the man who stands above us now,
While, so to speak, we tow the plough,
He will no doubt in another life,
Be born to hardship, want and strife.

And every soul will come to learn,
That with each life, we take our turn.
Walking paths that others tread,
Some paved with gold! Some paved with lead!

Richard John Scarr

13
MEDIUMSHIP

Linking to those who have moved over to the other side is an everyday occurrence. Since it is the spirit side of us that does the linking, I again stress, there is nothing in the least bit startling or dramatic about a spirit on this side of life linking with a spirit on the other side. After all, you can talk to your loved ones living on the other side of the world by telephone, and not give it a second thought. Well, that is all a medium is, a kind of telephone! And again, I cannot stress too highly — we all have that ability in us if we care to develop it! Mediums are not one of a kind! They are ordinary people like you and me, and so it is high time the mystique that seems to surround clairvoyance and healing etc. is stripped away, and it is realised our loved ones in the Summer Land are part of our everyday lives. Although the majority of people are simply not aware of the fact, our loved ones spend a great deal of time with us on this side. They are around us and know everything that is going on, and if we have problems, they do their best to help and influence the situation wherever and whenever they can.

This brings us to the point of 'speaking ill of the dead'! That saying came about because the dead are not dead, and the moment you start to talk about someone in the Spirit World, they know it. And then they will be with you instantaneously. If you are slagging them off, it might be as well to remember they will be standing there with you and listening to every word you say. On top of this, when we go over, we judge ourselves, and if we have anything to be ashamed of, or have done somebody wrong, we repent and need to be forgiven in order that we can move on. So it helps if we forgive those who have wronged us in any way before they moved to the other side. For there is nothing to be gained by holding on to a grudge, and we really do repent our sins once we get to the other side.

But, coming back to the business of awareness, I don't claim to know what the statistics are, but I would guess, for every medium born with awareness, there are probably hundreds who are born with absolutely no awareness at all and yet go on to become competent mediums by sitting in awareness groups and developing. I know of at least one household name who had little or no awareness when he began, and in fact did at least part of his training at my church, and he went on to become a very good medium, often to be seen on television. He wrote several books on the subject. He is no longer with us, having recently passed over. But I have no doubt once he has settled down to his new surroundings, he will find himself something useful to do, which will benefit the many.

Of course, there are good mediums and mediocre ones. Usually, mediocrity is caused by the medium wanting to run before he or she has learned to walk. Some fledglings, as trainee mediums are known, cannot wait to fly the nest, so to speak, and they take to the platform as working mediums before they are ready. The result is that they often find themselves struggling to bring someone through, or if they do make a link, they struggle with imparting the information they are being given, because they simply misinterpret it. The more they struggle, the more confidence they lose. Some mediums have been working the platforms for years. But because they left their circles before they were ready, they come across as mediocre, and remain so all their platform working lives.

But even fledglings have to be exposed to the public of course. How else are they to get the experience they need? They should be given every opportunity, but it should be done before invited audiences, such as family and friends. Either that, or the meeting should be advertised as medium and fledgling. Then the audience will know they will not be getting the abilities of a Colin Fry, a John Edward, a James Van Praagh or a Sally Morgan etc. in that fledgling, but one who is in the stages of training as a medium. But however it is advertised, they should always be accompanied by a proven medium, and this should continue until they have shown that they are ready and competent enough to take to the platform solo.

There are several ways in which a medium might work. Firstly, through clairvoyance, which means they see within their mind's eye what is being given to them, or by means of clairaudience which means they hear within their minds what is being said. They have to learn how to separate that which is being given by the person they are linking with from their own thoughts. One also receives symbols, which have to be interpreted. One also receives feelings, or clairsentience, as it is known. Often one feels the situation. But by whatever means a medium receives his or her information, quite frequently some of it at least becomes a matter of interpretation, and this is where one can easily make mistakes by putting the wrong interpretation on what is being given. So if a fledgling takes to the platform before he or she has mastered these abilities, then they can end up looking completely incompetent.

It is easy to misinterpret even the most obvious. I remember vividly sitting in an awareness circle many years ago. Apart from the medium, who was a very good friend, and one of the men in the group whom I knew slightly, the rest were complete strangers to me. While I was giving a message to another member of that circle, in my mind's eye I was looking down on an island surrounded by a sea which was of a beautiful shade of blue-green. I gave this information to the recipient which she readily accepted. My immediate interpretation was that I was being shown a tropical isle. I jumped to the conclusion that she had been away on some luxurious and exotic holiday. It turned out however, that she was a rep for a wine company and travelled regularly to Jersey, in the Channel Islands, in that capacity and had never been on a tropical isle in her life. As she said later, "Chance would be a fine thing!" And with hindsight, I could not remember being shown any palm trees, coconuts or hula girls etc. That is how easy it is to misinterpret and jump to the wrong conclusions when we are learning.

But it also goes to emphasise my point. The ability to develop awareness and be able to communicate with those on the other side is there in all of us. For although I was aware from a very young age that if I turned my hands palm uppermost, my hands would begin to tingle, sometimes to the point of pins and needles, and they would grow extremely hot (later in my teens it was explained to me by a medium that it was in fact healing energy that was causing this effect). To my knowledge I had absolutely no other form of awareness. I never had any invisible friends as a child, nor did I see spirits.

Now I have to admit that when I first sat in this particular awareness group in order to learn to communicate, although I was already a committed

Spiritualist, I was never really one hundred percent sure that I personally would ever be able to receive and pass on messages from those on the other side. For although I had learned many things while sitting in the circle, including being able to see someone's aura, I never really thought I would be able to tell other people things, and pass on information to them that in reality that I could not possibly know. But that is where I made a huge mistake!

If you are committed and truly want to work with the Spirit World, either as a working platform or as a healing medium (and the latter was my choice), then they will work with you! They do so through our guides. But it does not happen overnight. It takes time and dedication.

I have already mentioned one such attempt at passing on a message. But that was jumping the gun a little. Some weeks after beginning with this particular awareness group, the medium who was tutoring us pointed to me and said, "Stand up and give us a demonstration of your mediumship!"

To say that knocked me sideways is putting it mildly! And I immediately began to protest that there was no way I could do so, since I was not a platform medium and had never given a message from the other side in my life. Neither had I given any thought to the fact that sooner or later I would be asked to stand up in front of the group and do what I believed to be an impossibility on my part. It was then the medium spoke the words which I consider to be pure wisdom. Words which I have already quoted above. She said, "If you genuinely want to work with spirits and you prove to them you truly are dedicated, and that it is not just a passing fad, then they will be happy to work with you!" That brought home to me the fact that they were already working with me as a healer. But every circle I had been involved in, in the past, had been for the purpose of healing. I had never harboured any ambition to work on the platform as a clairvoyant, and so I had never before sat in a circle purely for developing clairvoyance. This was the first time.

Nevertheless, there was nothing I could do other than comply. And so I rose to my feet, knees knocking and stomach churning, and at the same time begging, 'Spirit, please help me!' Then I did something which I have rarely seen platform mediums do. I was so used to closing my eyes when laying on hands, I automatically closed them then. And it worked for me!

To my utter surprise, after a moment or two I found myself drawn to one of the women sitting there in the circle. I can't explain how I knew I should go to her. It was just a very strong feeling that drew me in her direction. And then I got another feeling. One that she was running, or had run away from something. I said as much to her, which she promptly denied. But the feeling persisted even more strongly. I asked her, "Have you recently moved home?"

I already knew the answer, although the lady was a complete stranger to me, and she replied, "Yes."

I then asked, "Did you move to get away from a bad situation?" Again, I already knew she had.

Again she replied, "Yes."

Now up to that point I had not been shown anything, neither had I heard voices, and yet I knew the information I was getting was true. Purely by feeling. Then I saw in my mind's eye the letter H. Big and jet black. I knew instinctively that this letter spelt bad news for her. I asked, "Why am I seeing the letter 'H'?"

She replied, "That is the person who did my head in!" and then again, I saw in my mind's eye two women standing side by side in a doorway, holding hands, one of which was the lady I was working with. But I saw no male. When I put this information to her, she made no reply. And yet I was still sure from what was being given to me that this lady was in a relationship with another woman.

It was at that point, that things took on a confusing aspect that might have thrown an experienced medium, let alone a raw beginner like me. In my mind's eye I could still see the two women standing there. But then I saw a child standing in front of them also. She was a pretty little thing of about five or six years of age, and she had a lovely smile. I asked, "Is there a little girl around you two?"

She replied, "Yes, she is my daughter." I then proceeded to describe the child. She had mousey-coloured hair, with a fringe, and I could see from a side view that her hair was cropped short at the back. And to all this information I got a yes. I was then taken on a trip through the child's bedroom and was shown stuffed animals and a fire screen etc, and I again received affirmatives. It was then that I saw the little island that I mentioned earlier, and upon which I had placed the wrong interpretation. This was the lady rep for a wine company.

When I had finished this first attempt at clairvoyance, I sat down feeling quite pleased with myself, because I had received a yes to practically everything I had given her, even though I had fluffed the tropical island bit. And yet I was, to say the least, still confused. For on the one hand the lady had a child, which indicated a relationship with a man. Yet in spite of this, I still had the strong feeling that I had been given in the first place that there was a loving relationship between the two women.

From this very first experience, I was to learn two things: the first being that although the Spirit World will never give the medium information that is of a real private nature, and will withhold all things that would embarrass the recipient, a gay relationship is not one of them. A loving relationship between two men or two women is as much accepted in Spirit as it is on this side. On several occasions I have witnessed a medium working with gay couples when relatives in Spirit have said how pleased they were that their loved one was in a happy relationship. On one of those occasions the person in Spirit thanked the partner for the love and support they were giving their own loved one.

The second thing I learned was to trust Spirit! For later I was to discover that everything I had been given and had passed on to the lady was gospel. I got to know her very well over the years that followed, and I only recount this now because the lady, who was a little reticent about her relationship all those years ago, is now quite open about her sexuality. The letter H, I now know was the initial for Helen, her ex-partner, apparently a very violent woman, and extremely bad news for this lady. It transpired that while Helen was at work one day, the lady and her daughter, with the help of her new partner, had upped sticks and had moved home exactly as it had been given to me.

There was a lovely sequel to this little episode. A few days after my first venture into clairvoyance, I was standing in the kitchen of our church. There is a window in one wall that looks out onto a hallway and the church entrance. I was talking to someone; I glanced up, and there, looking through the window at me, was a little girl. She had mousey-coloured hair with a fringe, and I recognised her immediately. It was the little girl, exactly as I had seen her in my mind's eye when reading for her mother. And then her mother appeared. She said, "I had to bring her to church in order to show you how accurate you were in describing her," which of course did wonders for my confidence. Since then, that child has grown into a lovely teenager.

I was also to learn along the way that the feelings at times that spirits give to the medium can be a bit off-putting. For instance, they sometimes pass on to the medium the symptoms of that by which they themselves passed over. Or the symptoms of something that the recipient is suffering. It only lasts momentarily, but suddenly the medium can find him or herself having problems with their breathing, because the person they are linking with passed with lung cancer, or was a chronic asthma sufferer. I was totally unprepared for it when it happened to me, and I thank God the experience was not too dramatic or painful.

Again, while sitting in circle, I was giving a message to a lady, and I saw a huge sunset. The panorama before my eyes could not have been anything other than an African safari. I gave that information and received a yes. The lady had indeed just returned from a safari. Then, to my consternation, I went completely deaf in my left ear. It was close to the point that I could not hear a single sound through it. Somewhat taken aback, I said, "I have gone completely deaf in one ear." The lady then explained that she too was suffering the same. She had picked up a bug whilst in Africa, and had completely lost the hearing in her left ear and was taking antibiotics for the problem. At that moment, much to my relief, my ear opened again and my hearing returned.

However, that is not as bad as, for instance, if one were linking with someone who has passed with bone or stomach cancer, and who momentarily passes on those symptoms to the medium, which is why you will sometimes hear a medium murmur, "Please take it away, and only give me the thought, not the symptoms."

I have been told by a couple of platform mediums that on occasions the symptoms passed on to them have been quite excruciating. But I should also explain. The person in Spirit is only passing on those symptoms as he or she remembers them. For on the other side, they are now fit and well, and in perfect health. Any problems their physical frame might have developed on the Earth Plane stay with the physical frame. There are no such problems in the Summer Land.

14
NOW I AM GONE

Do not grieve now I am gone
And do not wish me back again
I am at peace within the light
No longer sick, and free from pain.

Do not grieve now I am gone.
I am safe, and in God's keep.
I will be waiting in the Summer Land.
Be patient dear, and do not weep.

I am just a whispered word away.
More yet, a thought will do.
No matter be it night or day.
I will be there with you.

Speak to me, and I will hear.
No words of yours will fall.
Be they laced with joy or tears,
Upon deaf ears. I hear them all.

Dream of me. And when you wake,
Still feel my kisses on your face.
And wonder, did I really dream?
Or lay within my love's embrace?

Then, should you in my pillow find,
An indent that my head left deep,
Could there then, be any doubt,
I come to hold you in your sleep?

At times, when I am there with you,
And gently touch your hair.
You turn and softly speak my name,
For you know that I am there.

My dearest, we are still as one.
And the love we built our lives upon,
Still stands the test of time and pain.
Unbroken bond, though I am gone.

Richard John Scarr

15
ASKING FOR PROTECTION

As I have indicated, there is nothing spooky about Spiritualism. But it is true to say that before a medium begins to work, whether it is one who works on the platform giving messages or a healing medium who works in a healing clinic laying on hands, before actually beginning, they sit somewhere private and quietly open themselves up to Spirit, and as they do, they ask for protection while they are working. And when they have finished their work, they again sit quietly and close themselves down in order to sever that link with the Spirit World. But it is the medium, not the recipient of the messages or of the healing who needs that protection. The mediums are the ones making the link, and they are the ones open to any mischievous spirits that might be looking to make a nuisance of themselves.

People who were mischievous on this side, especially youngsters, take those foibles with them, as do we all. But I have never known that protection to fail, and if a medium does have a problem at any time, it can definitely be put down to not opening up properly and asking for that protection. However, having said that, I have experienced what can happen if having opened up, one fails to close down again after working, and so sever the link with the Spirit World.

The saying, 'Familiarity breeds contempt', is a true one.

I confess I was often somewhat lax at closing myself down again after working, and the result was, I would go home with the link still intact, and wide open to Spirit. I lost count of the number of times I was awakened in the night, the room filled with spirits, and all talking at once. It was literally like being at a football match. There were a couple of occasions when I woke from my sleep with this racket in my ears and I admit to getting quite cross, even to the point of yelling at them.

There were, however, far, far more nights when I was not actually woken up, but unbeknown to me, my sleep was being disturbed. I would get up in the mornings feeling very listless, and I would sit down and immediately fall asleep again. There came a time when I began to feel unwell.

As the weeks went on I really began to feel under the weather and completely run down and out of sorts. Yet it was nothing I could put my finger on. I was not in pain.

I had no coughs or sneezes. I just felt ill and lacked energy. All sorts of things ran through my mind, such as iron deficiency or anaemia. And of course, the big C! My doctor had prescribed various tablets, but I still felt yucky.

I finally got to the bottom of the problem when I had a private reading with a very good medium. Although I was expecting my wife and other members of my family to come through, it was in fact a total stranger who came through to me. It was explained to me that he came from one of the higher planes. He gave me a name which of course meant nothing to me. He then apologised for not bringing any of my loved ones through, and said he thought it was time he had a chat with me. He then went on to say, "You are not ill. You are drained!" He went on to explain that, because my spirit had been on this plane many times, and was an old hand at it, it attracted young spirits who were new to the Earth and who had come from a perfect environment where they had only been exposed to love and tolerance etc. But they now had to deal with everything our environment had to throw at them, both good and bad. And of course, some of it quite horrendous. So they needed reassurance from an older and more experienced spirit. I was conveniently supplying that spirit by failing to close down after healing, and was leaving the door wide open for them. Although I was under the impression I was having a good night's sleep, it was in fact a disturbed sleep. For night after night, week after week, these young spirits were coming in droves. He then explained that because I attracted young spirits, I should close down every night before going to sleep, regardless of whether I had been healing and had opened up or not.

Needless to say, that I followed his advice. Every night I lay and imagined myself completely cocooned in a white light. I then announced, "I am in my own space. Please do not enter unless I invite you in. But my own loved ones can enter whenever they wish."

I am pleased to say I started to feel better almost at once, and after a week or so I was back to my old self again. However, it was a good object lesson. For although I was only too well aware of the need to close down after healing, I had ignored that need to my cost. As it transpired, I now appreciate I need to close down every night, regardless of whether I have been working or not. I am quite sure there are others out there who, on reading this, will be able to relate to what I experienced.

One lady, a member of my church committee, had on one occasion been teaching at the London Spiritualist headquarters in Belgrave Square, London. At the end of the afternoon, she was so engrossed in conversation, she forgot to close down. Later while walking to the station on her way home, she passed a man walking in the opposite direction. As she did so, she experienced an overwhelming feeling of grief and depression, and she promptly burst into tears. Because she was still open to Spirit, she had picked up on the grief and the depression of the poor man she had passed, which again demonstrates the need to close down after working.

Only on one other occasion since have I experienced the football match-like racket, and that was when I forgot to close after healing, and then fell asleep before I had a chance to close down while in bed.

If you go to a Spiritualist church, or arrange for a medium to give you a private reading in your own home in hopes that a loved one will come through, then why should you, as the recipient, fear them, or need protection from them? If they loved you when they were on this side of life, then they go on loving you after they have made their transition. That love does not leave them just because they have made their journey home, and the same goes for friends and acquaintances. People who would never have done you any harm when they were on this side of life would certainly never harm you now that they are living in the all-loving, all-forgiving environment of the Spirit World.

Those loved ones who have made their transition home will still spend a great deal of their time on this side with you. Not a hundred percent of the time of course, for they also have other things to do. Not only do some of them take up opportunities that were never open to them here, but many work for the common good of others. It is all free will of course. My mother and my wife work with babies before they go to their nearest relatives to be raised in Spirit. Some people become healers on the other side. They become the opposite number to those healers working on this side, and are the ones who channel the healing energy through to the healers on this side, and by that means to the patient with whom the healer on this side is working and laying on hands.

When our loved ones are around us, they do their best to let us know they are there. One way is a show of sparks in the darkness — usually silver or blue. One of the most common methods they use is to give us the feeling that we have just walked into a cobweb — that itchy cobweb-like feeling that has you scratching your face or head. Another is the feeling that someone has gently touched your face or your hair, or you catch a sudden movement out of the corner of your eye that has you turning your head to see what it was. It is their way of drawing your attention. So if it happens to you, and you turn your head, don't forget to say hello, because you will be looking right at them. Talk to them as you would when they were on this side of life. They hear every word you say.

Neither do you have to be a medium in order to converse with your loved ones in the Spirit World. You can do so by using the cobwebs. I call it the cobweb feeling, because it feels as though something were crawling over your face and hair. It is in fact merely energy our loved ones' use. Sometimes it is a gentle feeling, but at times that energy can be quite fierce, and then, so is the itching. You can experiment during a quiet moment, especially when lying in bed with the light out. Talk to a loved one in Spirit. You don't have to talk out loud. You can do so with your thoughts. Ask him or her to give you the cobweb feeling. Sometimes the feeling begins immediately. At other times you might have to wait a minute or two. But once it starts, the feeling can grow in intensity. They are able to see a lot farther ahead than us, so you can ask them a question, and say, "If the answer is yes, give me the cobwebs." If you get the cobweb feeling, then it is a yes. If not then the answer is no.

But don't lose heart if it doesn't happen immediately. Some people find it takes several attempts over a period of time. In most cases lack of success is because they go into this experiment with negative feelings and doubts that it will happen for them. These negative thoughts can block the energy your loved one is putting out. Think positive! It will help your loved one to make that link. Believe me; your loved ones are just as anxious to link with you as you are with them.

But having said that, there are times when I too have problems linking with my wife. Sometimes I will ask her a question and get little or no response at all, while at other times the response is instantaneous. The words have barely left my lips when I am showered with energy, sometimes so fierce, the itch is unbearable and I have to scratch.

I believe (and this is an opinion that has been acknowledged by my wife with the cobwebs) that at times there is something going on within the Earth's environment that adversely affects our loved ones' ability to put out this energy, and so reduces it to the level where we can barely feel it, at times obstructing it completely, while at other times there is no impedance whatsoever.

So if you should have problems, remember that old adage, 'If at first you don't succeed, try, try, and try again.'

16
FOREVER US

I know you take comfort from knowing
I am with you, still love you and care.
But it is important too, that you understand,
I am always myself when I am there.

I am not that passing fluffy cloud,
Or blossom falling from a tree.
Nor music carrying on the breeze.
No, what I am, is me!

I am not the scented petals of a rose,
Bathed in early morning dew.
Or softly falling flakes of snow.
I am me! I shared my life with you.

I am the one who still adores you.
The one who loved you at first sight,
Who comes to kiss you every morning,
And again last thing at night.

And although we are parted for a while,
Our love lives on and on.
For the bond that bound us on the Earth,
Has never been so strong.

One day you will come to join me,
And I will be there to bring you through.
Forever Us! Now, and for always!
For I will still be me! And you, will be you!

Richard John Scarr

17
VISITS TO AND FROM OUR LOVED ONES

If you have lost someone to Spirit, the moment you think of them they will be there with you. And if you are grieving and crying, then they will be just as heartbroken, because they love you, and feel completely helpless and unable to help you in your grief. And more so of course, if it is a child. Eventually they will have to return to their own world, and if they leave you crying, especially if it is a parent, then they will be inconsolable on the other side. Those loved ones who are taking care of them will find it impossible to comfort them. That is why, when we lose someone, especially a child, we have to put on a brave face for their sake. If we manage to smile and behave normally, then they too will smile with us. How we behave has a direct bearing on how our loved ones react, and the mood in which they return to the other side. Try to remember too; it is you who is away from home, and not them! They are home and are waiting for your return.

When we come to this Earth, it is for a very brief stay, to learn and then to take that knowledge back home with us. The Spirit World is where we originated, and the world to which we return. Your loved ones are home, and they are living in a wondrous land, and in the bosom of all those family and friends who are also back where they belong. But your loved one will not be able to enjoy his or her return if you are grieving for them. The very last thing our loved ones want is for us to mourn their return home. They are not unhappy, and it is only when they see us cry that it makes them so. For apart from being able to visit you whenever they wish, they also have the added bonus of those occasions when you visit them in your sleep state. If you have lost a child, you will watch that child as he or she grows up in the Summer Land. How is this possible?

When we go sleep at night our spirit being leaves the human shell. Sometimes it will stay close by while the body is sleeping, while at other times it might go off visiting other places. Sometimes too, it is joined by another loved one or loved ones who are visiting from the other side. How many times have you awoken in the morning having had a dream about a loved one who has passed over, that was so vivid, it could almost be real?

I remember my sister Doris telling me of such a dream she had. She dreamed she and her husband, Harry, who had passed some nineteen years earlier, had visited the very first house they had lived in soon after they were married. She said it was so real, it was more like a memory than a dream. She went on to say that they did not actually enter, but had stood outside the front gate looking at the front of the house.

Now, had she said they had entered and had roamed over the house renewing old memories etc. I would have said it was a dream, and nothing more. But the fact that she insisted that they did not enter beyond the front gate told me it had not been a just dream, but that she really had made that visit with her husband. Spirit beings will never trespass where they do not belong. I am talking of those in the Spirit World. Not the paranormal, or Earth-bound ghosts who take up residence in someone's home. Our loved ones on the other side live by a very strict code of conduct. Although they have the ability to go absolutely anywhere, they wish, they will not violate other people's privacy. Since the people living in that house were neither family or even friends, neither Harry or my sister's spirit would have entered where they had no right to be. That property now belongs to someone else. The same goes for your privacy too. In those places where you need to be alone, you are alone, and they respect that privacy. They are very discreet.

But our own spirit beings do not always stay on this Earth Plane during the times when the earthly body sleeps. Often a loved one from the other side comes and takes it over for a visit to the Summer Land, and so we get to spend time with all those loved ones who have made their transition. And of course, we get to meet up with friends and people from the past whom we haven't seen in yonks, and no doubt some whom we were not even aware had passed over.

We also get to meet up with our pets which have passed over. I am not talking about something you keep in a bathtub, and would take your hand off given half a chance. Love transcends all things, and if you had a pet or pets whom you loved and who loved you, the relationship between you does not end when you or they pass over. If you go first, then they will follow you when it is their time. Or if they go first, then they will go to your nearest relative in Spirit, especially if it is a relative whom they knew. And when you go over, they will be there waiting for you.

I can think of nothing worse than losing a child. It is bad enough to lose a parent, a partner or a sibling, but to lose a child is far worse. If you have lost a child, even one who never saw the light of day, you do get to spend time with them on the other side. As the years go on, and they grow to adulthood in the Summer Land, you are a part of their growing up. It is rather like having a child away at boarding school whom you only see at end of term holidays, except that you get to see your child a lot more often. The problem is of course, you are not allowed to remember those visits while you still inhabit the Earth Plane. These memories are removed from your mind before you are returned to the sleeping form of your human shell, and there is a very good reason for this.

The land in which our loved ones live is literally a land of love, light and tolerance. A world of perfection, where there is no such thing as old age and everyone is in their prime and in perfect health. Where there are no aches or pains. No illness or loneliness. No way in which they can come to any harm. Where there is no decay, so nothing dies, and there is no dust or grime. Where the weather is perfection, and the colours and fragrance of the flowers and flora are enough to blow your mind.

Now imagine we were sick, or old and infirm. Especially if we lived on our own, and so we were lonely with it, and yet we retained the memory of all those visits to Summer Land. How long do you think it would be before we decided to help our own transition along? Not just us, but millions like us all over the world. That is why it is only when we make our final journey to the other side that we are allowed to remember all those visits, and so realise that we have continued to be a family, and have remained close to those we love in the Summer Land, regardless of the situation. So the child we lost to Spirit, perhaps thirty or forty years previously, and who is now an adult in the Spirit World, is in fact not a stranger to us at all, because we have continued to be a part of their lives, and they a part of ours.

When we first go to sleep at night it is usually after a tiring day. And so, for the first few hours our sleep pattern is quite deep, and we are not disturbed by the spirit side of us as it leaves our sleeping body. However, after a few hours our sleep pattern becomes lighter, and sometimes the returning spirit does disturb us as it re-enters our sleeping form. Have you noticed that each time you awake in the early hours, it is always around the same time, give or take ten minutes? Now you know why, and this will continue throughout your lifetime on this Earth.

When the spirit leaves the sleeping body it remains connected by what most Spiritualists think of as an invisible magnetic cord. This cord remains attached throughout the life span of the human body. Only when the human body can no longer sustain the spirit, and the spirit has to discard it, and permanent separation takes place, is that cord then severed. At this time, the spirit returns to the Summer Land to stay.

18
AN EVER-OPEN BOOK

Our life book began when I met you.
Countless pages recorded in time.
All the good things. Some bad. Some indifferent.
All the shared things that gave our lives rhyme.

You were more than my spouse, my dearest.
You were always the best friend I had.
I could not bear you be grief-filled and lonely,
And I give thanks it was I left here sad.

So I won't close the book on our story,
Or tuck it away up on the shelf.
I will let it lie open at the last page we turned,
For it reads: 'Both in sickness and health'.

Although a lifetime has passed, still our story,
Is here with me chapter and verse.
Our promise to love and to cherish,
Till death, and for better, or worse.

T'was never a lovelier book written!
And we wrote it as one, you and I.
Now I am waiting for its happy ending,
And that too will come, by and by.

Though sad and lonely without you,
I will not let our life story end.
For there is part of it still to be written,
The last chapter has yet to be penned.

Richard John Scarr

19
OUR PSYCHIC PETS

I feel I should give a mention to our pets. Although I am not a vet, and know very little about animals, I have had proof positive that our pet cats, and no doubt our pet dogs too, are most definitely psychic, and do see spirit beings.

Some three years after my wife made her transition, I was putting bread out for the birds late one evening. As I placed it in the bird house in my front garden, some of it dropped onto the lawn. As it did so, out of the corner of my eye I saw something dive out from under a bush, grab a piece of the bread and retreat back under the bush again. It was getting dark at the time, and so I approached the bush to investigate. As I did so, a marmalade cat ran out and jumped up onto the garden wall, some six feet high, where it stood, eyeing me fearfully. It was obviously a wild cat, of which there were several, living in a barn at a local farm. The mere fact that it was ready to eat dry bread showed it was very hungry indeed.

I went back indoors and opened a large tin of pilchards which I then placed on top of the wall. The cat waited for me to retreat, then made short work of the pilchards. The following day I bought some cat food, and sure enough, when I went out into the garden that evening, the cat was back sitting on top of the wall. And again, it waited until I had retreated before devouring the food. This went on for the best part of a week. Then one evening as I went out into the garden, the cat, which on this occasion had taken refuge under a parked car in the road, came running to meet me. As I placed the plate of food on the lawn, it began to rub itself against my arm, purring loudly.

It actually took several more evenings before I could entice it into my flat, and then it would only stay a short time, for it had obviously never been indoors before. It prowled about the living room and kitchen suspiciously. But nevertheless, I fitted a cat flap in a kitchen window and wedged it open, and I began to leave the food on the floor inside. The cat would come through, eat the food, then cautiously come into the living room, where it jumped up onto my lap. I had learned at the very outset to place a small rug on my lap, because Molly, as I had named her, had claws which had never been trimmed, and were like bunches of needles.

As time went on, she settled in. But whenever I had visitors she would race through the cat flap and disappear for hours. She was totally in fear of people, and even when a car went by, she would dive behind the settee. Neither would she allow herself to be picked up, and would struggle to be released. It took several years before she finally became domesticated enough to stay when I had visitors, and she will now let them make a fuss of her.

Then one evening while at the church, while receiving a message from my wife, the medium asked, "Who is Molly?" and I told her it was the cat. She then said, "Your wife says she arranged for Molly to visit you. She said the cat needed you. And you needed the cat!"

Molly has been with me now for some thirteen years. Often while on my lap she will suddenly raise her head and stare at a particular point in the living room, and I have absolutely no doubt she is seeing someone I cannot see. One evening during a message from my wife, she said that Molly could see her when she was there.

Just a few months ago, Molly began to act strangely in the kitchen. She would be eating her food, when suddenly she would dive out through the cat flap as though in a panic. When she returned, she would cautiously put her head through the flap and look around before actually entering. Each time I put food down for her she would constantly stop eating and look at some particular spot in the room, her tail twitching nervously.

One evening, as I placed her food on the floor, she was sitting on the kitchen table. But instead of jumping down to eat it, she sat there just staring down at the bowl, and only when I placed the bowl on the table would she eat. Even then, she would stop and stare at the floor nervously, her tail going to work, and that became the norm. She would only eat when her food was placed on the table.

My wife and I had lost two long-loved pets — a dog named Kim, which had to be put down because she developed cancer, and a cat named Susie which we had had for some sixteen years or so. I was now sure that either Kim or Susie, or both, were the cause of Molly's nervousness. For I know without doubt that both Kim and Susie visit me.

One morning, while pottering about in the kitchen, I bent to place something in the dust bag. As I did so, out of the corner of my eye I saw a cat walk past me from the cat flap. At the time, I never gave it a second thought. But when I walked back into the living room, Molly was lying fast asleep on the back of the settee, where she had been all morning. I suddenly realised too, that the cat I had just seen had been grey and white. Molly is marmalade. I realised it was Susie I had just seen, and I knew Kim also visited me. For I have been told on a couple of occasions by mediums that a dog was sitting at my feet.

The crunch came when, eating her food one morning on the table, she suddenly stopped eating and jumped to the floor and dived through the cat flap. I never saw her again all that day. Before going to bed I placed a bowl of food on the table for her to eat during the night, but when I got up the following morning,

Molly was sitting outside in the front garden, and the food was untouched. So I knew she hadn't been in all night. When I called to her, she cautiously poked her head through the flap, but would not enter. It took several attempts to persuade her to come through. I was now more than ever sure it was the spirits of our passed-over pets that were scaring her.

This went on for some four or five weeks. Some mornings were easier to get her to enter than others. There were days when I would call her and she would poke her head through the flap, and then point-blank refuse to enter. So it was obvious she was seeing something that frightened her. Other mornings she would look around and then enter, but hesitantly. I was at my wits' end as to what to do about it. Then one morning I suddenly found the answer. I am still not sure whether the inspiration was mine, or whether it was passed to me from the Spirit World. But I suddenly found myself demanding in a very strict voice, "Spirit, be gone! And only come when Molly is not here. This is Molly's home!"

I still find it hard to believe, but as the day went on, Molly came and went through the cat flap quite normally. When I placed food on the floor, she ate it without any nervous staring around, or twitching of her tail. That evening as I sat watching television, the living room door opened and in walked Molly, and she jumped up onto my lap for a cuddle before disappearing out into the night to do what cats do at night. She hadn't done that in weeks.

Everything has now returned to normal. When I get up in the mornings, if the weather is good, there is no sign of Molly. But the food I left out overnight is gone. But if it is chilly or raining, I find her curled up on the mat in the kitchen, fast asleep. Why this problem suddenly developed after all these years, I have no idea. But it has now resolved itself, thank goodness. So if you are having the same problems with a pet, after having lost long-loved pets, try the same technique. It worked a treat in my home.

20
THE HALLS OF REST

No one makes their journey home alone. Neither could they! And our loved ones in the Summer Land know the exact moment we are to make our transition, and there is always one or more present to take us over when that time comes.

The spirit side of us, when we leave the physical frame, is as you might imagine, very light. A loved one simply cradles us in their arms and takes us home through the veil and directly to the halls of rest, or as some Spiritualists call them, the halls of healing, where we are laid upon a couch. There we are taken care of by loving and kindly people, who are not doctors or nurses as such, although they might well have been so when on this side of life. But there is no need for doctors or medical staff as such, because there are no illnesses or medical problems on that side of life. They are strictly volunteers who take care of us while we enjoy a healing sleep. It is their way of working for the common good of others.

How long we sleep will depend entirely on how long and how much we suffered before making our transition. If one suffered a long drawn out illness before passing over, then the spirit side of us will need a longer healing period of recovery than say, someone who passed over having had a heart attack, which would have been a quick passing. Either way, we will awake to find ourselves surrounded by loved ones, for they will have been expecting us, and at least one of them would have been involved in bringing us over.

For those of us who are part of the Spiritualist movement, it is of course no surprise, for we are expecting them to be there. But for those with no knowledge of the other side — or who simply do not believe life goes on and that death is the end of life — then for them, it will be a most joyous awakening.

Some years ago, I received a phone call from someone who had once been very close, and who was terminally ill with lung cancer. She was terrified. I tried to calm her by explaining that she was not going to die, and could not do so, not even if it was her wish. But she was not even prepared to talk about it, or listen, such was her fear. She put the phone down on me. Some five or six months after her passing I received a message from her. She was over the moon, and so excited to be making contact, and yet she still found it hard to believe that she really was very much alive and in such a wondrous place. And, most importantly, she was fit and well and was a young woman again. She went on to say that she appreciated that I had been trying to help her. She acknowledged that if she had been able to listen to me, her passing would have been so much easier. As it was, her sister, Rose, had been there at the moment of the separation, and had taken her over to the halls of rest. I can only imagine her reactions when she awoke to find herself surrounded by all her loved ones.

She, like the rest of us, had of course been over before. But the memory of our previous lives and our return to the Summer Land is removed each time we come back here, although there are a few people who are allowed to remember, in order to spread the word about the 'Hereafter'.

But of course, we cannot be in two places at once. We cannot be here on the Earth in a human host body while at the same time residing in the Summer Land with those loved ones from a previous life. So once we take the decision to return to the Earth Plane for another life span, we cease to be a part of our family in the Spirit World. But that is an accepted part of life on the other side. Unlike the inhabitants of this world, those we leave behind in the Spirit World do not weep or grieve for us; for they know that far from dying, we have just begun a completely new life.

Time and again people come through who say, "When I was on the Earth, I would not have gone within a mile of a Spiritualist church." And some say they did not believe in life after death. Well, they believe in it now! If there are any among you who do not believe, then you are simply doubting yourselves. For whether you like it or not, you are part of

Spiritualism. You cannot but help be part of it, because you are a spirit in a physical frame.

But unfortunately, the human part of us being what it is, there are always going to be those who knock and put down that which they do not understand. You can often find them online. Someone will make a comment about their spiritual beliefs, or perhaps about a meeting with a clairvoyant, and up pops the authority on the subject, and out pours invective and malicious diatribe, and we are treated to remarks like, "What a load of old cobblers! Just a bunch of con artists taking idiots for a ride! The only place we go when we die is down in a bloody big hole, or in the oven!"

Quite apart from being completely misinformed, this kind of outburst is spiteful and totally ignorant! In that ignorance they attempt to tear apart other people's beliefs, and that which brings them comfort and takes away the fear of death — those countless number of people who are terminally ill, and yet can face their transition because of their faith in life after death. It is this faith that these ignorant people attack. And yet, make no mistake about it, how their thinking would change if they found themselves in the same position, and facing their last days on this Earth. Especially when waking from a restless sleep in the early hours, lying there with their thoughts and feeling so alone, and with the knowledge they are not long for this world. I have no doubt at all that the very thing they were so disdainful about — life after death — they would pray with all their hearts that it really did exist! That, they can take comfort in. It does!

One of the most enjoyable things about being in the Summer Land is the fact that they have the best of both worlds. They live in a world that can only be described as perfection, and when they wish, they can visit this side of life in the wink of an eye. They are aware the moment someone here starts to think about them. They hear our every thought, which means we can talk to them even in a doctors' waiting room, or in a library, without uttering a word.

When they first arrive in the Spirit World everything is new to them, even though they have already been there at least once before. But now, having arrived back, they are starting anew, and so they have to learn everything all over again. And that includes coming back through the veil on a visit, or linking with a loved one on this side through a medium. They receive the help of someone who has been over there for a while, and whom Colin Fry used to term an 'enabler', to show them the ropes. However, it does not take them long before they are ready to fly solo, so to speak. In the meantime, when we get that first, and even a second message from them, it is usually with the assistance of that someone who is helping them, and is bringing them through. Sometimes that someone might not be well known to us — perhaps it is someone we met only briefly. Yet in the first instance it will be the enabler the medium will link with. Then having obtained his or her name, the medium will tell you who it is he or she is linking with. If that name means nothing to you, then you automatically jump to the conclusion the medium has come to the wrong person, and should be with someone else, and so you reject the person she is linking with. At that point the medium will have no choice but to break the link. That in fact happened to me.

My wife passed in January 2004. She had a kidney stone and was in a lot of pain. On December 27th 2003 I took her to our local hospital. But there were problems right from the start. My wife had a very bad heart which in turn resulted in a dangerously low blood pressure. A few days after arriving there, a woman was brought in suffering from a very bad cold bug, and needless to say, it spread through the ward. My wife took the bug and it turned to pneumonia, and she was taken to the intensive care unit. From then on everything went downhill. Her heart, kidneys and liver began to fail and they were unable to stabilise her. I was called to the hospital and told to expect the worst, and she passed that same evening.

As I said earlier, being a Spiritualist, and so knowing exactly where our loved ones are and that they are very much alive, does not prevent us from missing them and feeling lonely. So, mainly in order to get out of my flat for a while, one Sunday evening I

wandered into one of the local Spiritualist churches —
the church of which I was later to become so much a
part. Eventually the medium on the platform came to
me. She asked me if I could take the name of Anne.
Although I racked my mind, I could think of no one of
that name whom I knew at that time, either in Spirit or
on the Earth Plane, and so I said no. The medium then
said the lady she was linking with was talking about
someone with a speech impediment. The only person I
had met with such an impediment was the son of a
friend of my brother. The poor chap had an intellectual
disability, together with a bad speech impediment. But
since I barely knew him, I disregarded him, for they
were after all, friends of my brother. With me not
being able to accept this lady, the medium very
reluctantly broke the link.

Later that night I spoke to my brother on the
phone and mentioned what had happened at the
Spiritualist church. His reaction was one of surprise.
He said that his friend's wife, the mother of the man
with the speech impediment, and who had died the
previous year, was in fact named Anne. He also said
that my wife and I had met her once at a barbecue
which he had held, and only then did I vaguely
remember meeting the lady, though the name still
meant nothing to me. But I was now in no doubt that
this was indeed the lady who had come through.

The following Sunday I again went to the church.
On this occasion it was a different medium on the

platform. But yet again, during the course of the evening the medium came to me, and once again I was asked if I could take the name of Anne. This time I acknowledged the lady, and the medium then told me that she had not come through for herself, but had brought someone else through, which of course, turned out to be my wife. And so, I received the first of many, many messages to come. On one occasion my wife too acted as a go-between, and brought someone else through.

One Sunday morning I was playing in a bowls match. A friend, a fellow bowler named Ray, whose wife Ruth had passed a few months previously, was watching. During a break in the match, he asked if I was going to my church that evening. I told him I was, and he asked if he could accompany me, to which I readily agreed. My wife's name is Berenice Helen, but I call her either 'Bell' or 'Berry' for short. That afternoon I looked at my wife's photograph and said, "Bell, if you can possibly bring Ruth through this evening, it will make Ray a very happy man." I had no doubt whatsoever that my wife had been with me while I was at the bowls club, and so would already be aware that Ray would be joining me that evening at the church. I had little doubt too, that bringing Ruth through was already her intention anyway, although my wife had never met either Ruth or Ray while on the Earth, my wife not being a bowler.

That evening as Ray and I sat together in the church, the medium, whom I knew, looked at me and said, "Why am I hearing little bells ringing above your head, Richard?" and I explained to her my wife's name was Berenice, and one of the names I had for her was 'Bell'. The medium then said, "She's here! But she has not come through for you." Then she looked at Ray and said, "Bell has brought your wife through," and she then proceeded to give him a message from Ruth.

The fact that Bell had never met Ruth during her life on Earth was no obstacle. It was proved to me, soon after Bell passed, that looking up people they had never met before on this side of life is no problem at all. Shortly after Bell had made her transition, I read an article in the Daily Mail written by a columnist who had recently lost his wife, Audrey. If I remember rightly the article was called 'Life without Audrey' or 'Life after Audrey' or something very similar. In this article he said he found himself looking at car number plates, and was surprised how many vehicles he found crossing his path, so to speak, with the number plate containing the letters AUD, for Audrey, and he felt it was her way of letting him know she was OK, and had arrived in the Spirit World safe and sound.

From then on, I found myself doing the same thing. I was amazed at the number of vehicles that crossed my path containing the letters 'BEL" or "BS' or 'BHS': Berenice Helen Scarr. I also found myself noticing plates with the letters AUD for Audrey, which

I would read out aloud too. So you can imagine then my amazement when one evening at the church, a medium informed me, "Your wife said she has met Audrey!"

As I mentioned earlier, a medium is something like a telephone, conveying messages from someone on the other side to someone on this side. So when people attend a Spiritualist meeting where a medium is in attendance, their loved ones in Spirit are aware of it immediately, and they all want to come through and make a link with those family members and loved ones present. So they vie with each other to grab the medium's attention, and it is those with the strongest personality that win. Although that is not to say that it isn't done in a friendly fashion, or that they won't all take a back seat when it is necessary. If for instance someone at that meeting is grieving badly, then those in the Spirit World will know it, and they will ensure the loved one of that person, has access to the medium and so is able to pass a message to the one who's grieving.

21
IF I HAD ONLY KNOWN

I won't pretend I was not scared,
Because I felt so all alone.
No one could make the journey with me.
I had to make it on my own!

I had always placed my trust in God,
But when your time is drawing near,
Especially in the wee small hours,
You just can't push away those fears.

I so much wanted to believe,
What I'd been told was true.
That I was moving to another life,
But still those doubts came flooding through.

But there, I made my first mistake,
For no one journeys on alone.
A loved one from the other side,
Always comes to take us home.

If I had known what I know now,
I would not have lost a moment's rest.
It is far the easiest thing I have done,
And certainly, the best!

For I woke up in a wondrous world,
Surrounded by my loved ones too.
All my kin, and all my friends,
Who had also made the journey through.

Fit, and full of energy,
Young again, and in our prime.
I promise this awaits you too.
So when it comes, don't fear your time!

Richard John Scarr

22
GRIEF

Grief for those who do not understand Spiritualism is a devastating experience. Especially for those who believe that death is the end of everything, and there is nothing beyond the grave or the crematorium. Even for a lifelong Spiritualist, losing a loved one is bad enough, for even knowing their loved one has not died, but has merely made his or her transition home to the Summer Land does not prevent their sense of loss, or stop them from missing that loved one and feeling lonely without them.

For a wife or husband who has perhaps spent two thirds of their lives with their spouse, only to find themselves alone, a widow or widower, Spiritualist or not, their loved one is no longer with them and the house is just empty. It is every bit as heart-breaking to see their partner's clothes hanging in the wardrobe, knowing they will never wear them again, and be aware — of course — that they must eventually be disposed of. When evening comes and they close the curtains and find themselves alone looking at the empty chair where they were so used to seeing their spouse sitting, being a Spiritualist will not help to hold back the tears. But nevertheless, for someone with little or no knowledge of transition, the loss of a loved one is infinitely worse.

It will not be long before the Spiritualist will seek the help of a Spiritualist church and their mediums in order to link them with their loved one on the other side, and so draw comfort from that link. They will continue to do so through all future links until acceptance comes. But for the uninitiated who feel nothing but total loss, it is the beginning of a long journey through grief.

Grief can affect people in different ways, but I think the most common is at first, complete shock and a dazed feeling — inability to accept the fact that their loved one has gone. This is followed by pain and heartache — the feeling that their world has collapsed, and for many, the feeling that they can't, or don't want to go on. This is accompanied by endless nights of crying themselves to sleep, and some, like myself, take solace in the bottle in order to get through the days and nights.

This phase is usually followed by anger — anger at God for having taken their loved one, and then angry at their loved one for having left them alone. Then finally comes guilt! They find themselves remembering things they had said or done, no matter how small. Those little things magnify in their minds until they have grown out of all proportion, and they begin asking for forgiveness of their loved one.

In those early days too, it is difficult to go anywhere without being reduced to tears. For no matter where they go, it holds memories. They have been there with their loved one. Even going to the local supermarket where they have shopped for years can be an ordeal. As a result, where possible, they find themselves avoiding those places where, in the past, they had spent many pleasant hours with their loved one.

But without any doubt, for those who do not understand that life goes on in the Summer Land, it is an even longer journey until they finally make it through their grief. For that reason alone, I hope these pages will help those people to understand their loss is only a temporary one, and they will be reunited with those who have gone before.

While we are on the subject of grief, I think this would be an ideal moment to talk about what is probably one of the most painful stages of losing a loved one — the death bed, and watching a loved one pass.

Those who have experienced this will know just how heart-breaking it can be to watch someone you love take their last breath. Because at that point, all you are aware of is your loved one lying there unmoving and no longer breathing, and that can be absolutely devastating. Yet, if you only knew, and could see what was actually taking place around that bedside at the precise moment of your loved one's passing, then perhaps it might help to dull a little of the pain and grief. So let us see if we can re-enact the moment of a passing.

As I have already mentioned, the spirit is the source of life for the human body. It is only when it leaves the body that the human side of us expires. And this means literally that the spirit side of us takes its leave of the human shell before the shell takes its last breath. So let us imagine for instance that it is a parent, or a grandparent lying there. At the point when they appeared to be breathing their last, the spirit side, the real him or her, would, unbeknown to you, be standing there with you also watching what is taking place, and without any doubt, they would have their arm around you, trying to comfort you. Not only this — he or she would also be accompanied by at least one or more of your loved ones who had come from the other side in order to take them over. I say at least one, because sometimes it might be more. They too would be doing their best to make the moment easier for you, and yet unable to let you know that they are present, and that no one is dead, other than the human shell, which was created solely for the purpose of playing host to your loved one while he or she was on the Earth Plane.

So then, although you are under the impression that you are alone with the body of your loved one, there could in fact be quite a crowd around you, including your loved one. All you actually have is the cast-off human shell he or she had decided it was time to discard, and which, if they had been suffering, they would have been very relieved to be rid of!

The same applies to all our loved ones when they pass, whether it be someone who lives to old age or someone who came to this Earth with a shorter life span ordained. They too will be standing with you watching from the bedside, and accompanied by another, or other loved ones from the other side. If it is a young child you have lost, then a loved one from the other side, perhaps a grandmother, will be there with you and will be holding the child in her arms, ready to take it over.

This then, is the scene that is played out every time somebody passes in the orthodox manner. No one goes over alone! However, as far as being aware of actually leaving the earthly frame is concerned, there are exceptions to the rule. On several occasions, people from the other side have said that before they passed over, they fell asleep and then felt as though their body were trying to rise from the bed. Then the next thing they knew, they were waking from their sleep in the halls of rest to find themselves surrounded by those loved ones who went before. My own sister, Vera, went in this way, as I mention at the end of these pages.

I believe that in cases where there has been painful suffering over a long period before passing, the spirit becomes so drained and tired, they go into a deep sleep before their transition, and so are not really aware of the separation as it takes place. They are then carried over by a loved one from the other side, to the halls of rest.

Shortly after my wife passed, she came through and verified that at her passing, she had been standing with me watching her earthly shell take its last breath. Her concern had been solely for me, and how I was feeling, and she thanked me for taking good care of her during her illness. She also thanked me for holding her hand during her last moments on the Earth Plane, and for letting her go quietly and peacefully.

The only time the scene as described above is not played out is when the spirit is expelled from the human shell suddenly and violently, such as in cases of instantaneous death where it happens in a flash, as with a car or motorcycle crash or an explosion. In these cases, it can be quite bemusing for the spirit side of those who go in this way.

I remember one young chap who was killed as the result of a motorcycle accident, saying that as he approached a corner, he knew he was traveling too fast. Then the next thing he knew, he was standing bemusedly looking down at his own body lying on the pavement where it had come to rest. Other traffic was stopping and people were gathering round the scene, but no one was taking any notice of him. It was a shock to realise that he was in fact no longer one of these living beings, and yet he was still alive, even though these people could not see him. He simply stood there, not knowing what he should do or where he should go. And then his grandfather appeared at his side and placed an arm around his shoulders, and took him through the Veil. At the time he too jumped to the conclusion that people who pass have no solid body, because no one had been aware of his presence. But he now realises, the reason he could not be seen by those who had stopped at the scene of the accident was because he was still in spirit form, and had not yet reached the Summer Land, where he again took on a solid form.

It had happened so fast, even his loved ones on the other side were caught napping. This sort of thing happens very frequently during wars. People who meet their end by sudden and violent means such as explosions etc. sometimes find themselves wandering, not knowing what has happened to them. And because their loved ones on the other side have been taken by surprise too, they sometimes arrive on the scene to find their loved one on this side has wandered off. There are many, many lost souls wandering during wars and even at other times too for various reasons. But fortunately, there are people on both sides of life who specialise in rescuing these Earth-trapped spirit beings, and help them to make their transition to the other side to be with their loved ones.

Before we leave this chapter, I would like to stress once more that whatever it is that takes your loved ones home, to the Summer Land, they do not carry the cause home with them. Nor do they carry any injuries or scars. All that is left behind with the earthly remains on this side of life.

So then, if your loved one passed with an illness that took its toll on his or her human frame, leaving it looking desperately ill and ravaged etc. as some illnesses and diseases tend to do, or if they passed as a result of some bad injury, I promise you faithfully; he or she returned home to the Summer Land looking in the pink, and as fit as a flea!

23
WHERE LIFE BEGINS AGAIN

I can truly say I have made it back,
And I have journeyed through my grief.
But it took time to reach where I am now,
For the journey was not brief.

And although, gradually acceptance came,
There is still a part of me
That is ever turned towards the light.
And wishing it could be.

In the land of new beginnings,
Where life begins again,
And where the one I cherish waits for me,
And the bond we forged, remains.

And though each day seems a lifetime,
I will wait here patiently,
Knowing that, when my time comes,
We will share eternity.

Until then, somehow, I will muddle through,
Although I really don't know how.
And my life will have no meaning till
I am with my love, where she is now.

Richard John Scarr

24
HEALING AND ABSENT HEALING

While sitting in the circle I mentioned earlier, I did of course continue healing. But once I had finished with the circle, the opportunities to practise clairvoyance just weren't to be had. Not that I am in any sense a platform medium. Healing was and is my first love, and that which I have strived over the years to develop. So, sitting in an awareness circle once every few years in order to develop clairvoyance is not conducive to making a good clairvoyant. Although at times, I wish I had dedicated more time to it. One has to apply oneself long and hard in order to develop the kind of awareness needed to make the kind of platform medium people would want to come and see, and I would not want to be a mediocre medium. While actually sitting in a circle amid the psychic energy being generated by those sitting with me, the evidence I receive and pass on is extremely good, but once I have left the circle, although I get the odd message now and then, it is only when they themselves have something they want to pass on to me. Or when my wife is feeling mischievous.

For instance, one Sunday I was running late for church and I was down to chair for the medium of the day. I snatched my socks off the bed and hurried out to the kitchen, intending to place them in the washing machine. But absentmindedly I tossed them into the kitchen bin. Realising immediately what I had done, I retrieved them again and placed them in the washing machine. As I made to leave, I had barely reached the kitchen door when within my mind I heard a giggle, and my wife's voice, as clear as a bell, said, "You were right the first time, my old darling!"

She has not let it rest there. On a couple of occasions, she has mischievously raised the subject of those socks while I have been sitting among the congregation at the church. The medium would ask, "Why is your wife talking about a pair of socks?" and I would then have to recount to all those present of the time I threw my socks into the bin, and of my wife's considered opinion that this was the right place for them.

That is not the only time she has demonstrated her sense of humour. On another occasion I awoke with pains in my knuckles and wrists, and even my kneecaps. As the day went on, the pains grew more severe. I looked at my wife's photo and said, "I think I must have something wrong with my blood, Bell. I have pains working around my body." I became fearful that my time had come. However, by the evening the big toe on my right foot became painful and was

117

extremely hot, and I realised it was gout working around me. I had forgotten that you can get gout in any joint in your body. I took some gout tablets over the next few days, it cleared up and I forgot the incident. But my wife had not.

It must have been a week later, and again while at the church, the platform medium asked, "Why is your wife asking me to tell you, 'You have not got one foot in the grave, my old darling'?" I then had to explain to the congregation about the time I had jumped to the conclusion that I was at death's door. But it turned out be gout!

'Old darling' is what she used to call me at times when she was here. But on two separate occasions she came through with a message for me, and said, "This time I won't call you my old darling, because when you come over in your sleep state you are not much more than a boy. You are only about twenty-one, and you are lovely." I suppose, after seeing me as I am on this side of life, in my eighty-ninth year as I write this, when I go over in my sleep state I must look little more than a boy to her. But equally, she is of course of the same age on the other side. A mere girl.

But I might even yet, dedicate myself to the development of clairvoyance, and then do a bit of platform work. After all, I have put in the groundwork over the years, so I know those on the other side will be willing to work with me. However, even if I were good at it, the passing on of messages from the other side, to the patient during healing, is taboo! A complete NO-NO! Quite rightly too, because the lovely people we work with on the other side, who are our opposite numbers and who channel the healing energy through to us on this side, need a clear field in order to do their job, as we do also. And those are the only spirit beings who should be linking with the healer on this side.

Unfortunately, however, on occasions a spirit side family member or friend of the patient receiving the healing will try to use the link forged to get a message through to them. Imagine you are on a phone passing important information on to someone, and someone else comes on the line talking over you, completely obstructing what you are trying to say. That is exactly what happens when an opportunist on the other side tries to use the healing link to get a message through to the person you are working with. That opportunist completely obstructs the healer on the other side, and in so doing, obstructs the healing energy that is being channelled through, and, of course, obstructs the healer on this side from receiving that energy.

No healer this side should ever pass on a message given in this way, but instead, in the kindest way possible, break the link with the opportunist, making it clear to them that when they trespass during a healing session, they are obstructing the healing their own loved one or friend should be receiving. If an opportunist succeeds once in getting a message through in this manner, he or she might try it again and again. I have absolutely no objections to the spirit loved ones of patients letting me know they are there in some other way, for instance by placing a symbol of some sort before my eyes, or using any other method, just as long as they do not try to get online, so to speak.

Some time ago I was giving healing to a young woman who had recently lost her father. She was grieving for him very badly, and had lost a lot of her hair. Suddenly the statuette-like symbol of a lion was placed in front of my eyes, which were closed at the time. The statuette remained there during the whole of the healing, and there was nothing I could have done to remove it. Not that I tried, or wanted to. For I had no doubt it was connected with the young woman in my chair. When the healing had finished, I asked the young lady if she had the statuette of a lion in her home, to which she replied, "No."

At that moment her mother, who had also been receiving healing, joined us. I repeated the question, explaining that I'd had this lion with me all through the healing. The mother shook her head. Then she said, "But my husband's birth sign was Leo the lion!"

The statue of the lion had been her husband's way of letting his daughter know he was there, and he had very sensibly done so without obstructing either me or the healers on the other side. For of course he knew I would query the symbol he had placed before my eyes.

I am pleased to say the young lady took comfort from this, and she came for healing again the following week. I was able to inform her that her father was once again with us all through the healing.

Some spirit relatives of those who come for healing will go to remarkable lengths to let their loved ones know they are present. On one occasion while I giving a patient healing, another patient, to whom I gave healing quite regularly, came into the healing sanctuary. She opted to wait until I had finished rather than go to one of the other healers. After a while I became aware of her sobbing. Knowing she had lost her husband some six months previously, I assumed she was just having a bad moment. When I had finished with my patient, the lady took her place in the chair, still sobbing. I began to offer her words of comfort, but she shook her head and said, "While you giving that patient healing, I looked at you, and as I did so, my husband's face became superimposed over yours. He smiled at me, then it slowly changed back to your face."

This then, was an act of involuntary trance mediumship, of which I had been totally unaware. But as I placed my hands on her shoulders, I became aware of a gentle pressure on the backs of my hands, as though someone had placed their hands over mine. At the same time, the lady stiffened as though she had received an electric shock, and she again began to sob uncontrollably. I continued with the healing, and when I had finished, she told me that, although she could not put the feeling that went through her into words, she knew her husband had been part of that healing.

But this was not the first time I had been used in this way. On another occasion I was chairing a Sunday service, the last forty minutes of which is given over to clairvoyance. When the service had finished and we were having a cup of tea, a medium who had been sitting in the congregation asked me if I practiced trance mediumship. I told her I did not. She then said, at one point when the medium on the platform was giving someone in the congregation a message from a loved one, my face was transformed and another face was superimposed over it. It had lasted for some ten seconds or so, and then it had changed back to my face. But again, I had not been aware of it.

As I have already emphasised, we all have the ability in us to become a healer if we so wish. However, we do not need to lay on hands, or sit in a circle in order to learn healing. Each and every one of us has carried out healing of a kind at some time or other. For instance, how many times have you stopped to chat to someone whom you knew had been ill, and done your best to boost their morale and uplift their spirits, by telling them they were looking in the pink, and when taking your leave, said to them, "I wish you better!" That is healing! Or when you stop to give someone a word of encouragement because you know they have problems, or are grieving or when you sympathise and offer them your sincere best wishes, and tell them they have been in your thoughts. That is healing!

Healing can take many forms. If you want to be a healer but do not want to lay on hands or sit in a circle, then it is open to you to become an absent, or distant healer. And please believe me, this form of healing is every bit as important and effective as the healing carried out by healers who make a link with a healing spirit while laying on hands. So if you want to heal in this way, then make no mistake about it, those lovely people on the other side will work with you. They simply do so in a different way to which they work with the rest of us. We work with them by making a link so that the patient sitting in the chair receives healing direct. But when sending out absent healing to people you know who are in need, it is done in their absence, and from a distance, either through thought or word of mouth. The method you use is up to you. I can assure you every thought and every word you utter during each absent healing session is heard by healing spirits, and is acted upon. Just because you have not sat in a circle, or have not been trained as a healer, this does not mean healing spirits will not work with you. They will! You do not need training as such for this kind of healing. Yet the importance of absent healing must not be underestimated!

I am privileged to know several people who have almost made a career of absent healing. They have never sat in a circle, or trained to be a healer, and yet they do as much good work and are as much recognised as healers by the Spirit World as any of us who lay on hands. How then, do you become an absent healer?

Sending out absent healing can be said to be on par with praying. The difference is, you do it in private, and prepare yourself before you actually start the healing session. It is always best where you can sit in total silence away from other people; always switch off the phone so that you will not be interrupted. Sit and relax your body and lay your hands on your knees, with palms turned uppermost. Then close your eyes and allow yourself to breathe steadily. At that point, let all other thoughts go and think only of healing spirit. Then ask, "Dear God, please open me up to healing spirit," and I promise you those lovely people on the other side who will be working with you will know immediately that you are in touch, and will hear your every word. Trust me!

Once you have gone through the opening up part, then send your healing thoughts and prayers for everyone you know by name who is in need of healing, and for all sick and suffering everywhere. Think of those in hospitals, clinics and those too who are terminally ill in hospices. The list is endless.

When you have finished your absent healing, it is important that you again sit quietly and ask, "Dear God, please close me down again and sever the link." Or you can close down yourself simply by following the procedure mentioned earlier in the chapter 'Asking For Protection'.

You can set your own healing times, as frequently as you wish. If you hold regular absent healing sessions, then you will of course become known to those on the other side as a healer, and they will look forward to joining you at these session times. One thing I can promise you, and that is, your healing prayers will not go unheard. But do not feel you have failed if, for instance, you send out healing prayers for someone who does not recover. Remember, we all have an allotted time to go, and we all must have the means by which to leave this plane. So if it is the time for the person you are sending healing prayers and thoughts for to make their transition, then they will move over to the other side regardless. But at the same time, do not doubt that your healing made his or her passing a whole lot easier. Healing spirits will see to that. So your healing has not failed, and the person you were sending out healing for will know what you did for them once they reach the other side, and they will be grateful to you.

There are other ways to become a healer too; one of those ways is to become a hospital visitor. No doubt you yourself have either been in hospital, or have been visiting someone, and have become aware of some poor soul who never received a visitor, and who either spent the whole visiting period lying with the blankets pulled up to their chin as though asleep, or just lay there watching others receive them. Becoming a registered visitor, and spending even one afternoon a week sitting talking to one or two of these patients, helping to take away that feeling of loneliness and isolation, is a great form of healing. So too, if you have the heart for it, is becoming a hospice visitor (there are just as many lonely hospice patients who have no one to visit them). For it has been my experience that the majority of these patients themselves sit and chat quite normally. If you understand Spiritualism, and provided the patient is quite happy to chat about the subject, you can make him or her understand that they are not going to die, but are merely going to move from life to life, and if, in so doing, you help to make that person's transition easier, then that is healing at its very best!

When we are born, everyone is allocated a guide, and that guide remains with us during the whole of our lifetime. Their job is to try to keep us on the straight and narrow. However, when we work for Spirit, we are often allocated other guides who also help with our work. Some people, like myself, have three or four guides who work with us at various times. Apart from my own guide, who is a North American Indian, I have a Jewish rabbi who works with me from time to time — also a Chinese gentleman and Buddhist monk. But for the most part, I rarely know which one is working with me when I am healing. On one occasion when I had finished giving a patient healing, he asked me if I was Jewish. He said that during the healing he saw the Star of David in front of his eyes. So I assume it was the rabbi who was working with me at that time.

My healing colour is that of the heart chakra — a beautiful shade of emerald green, which comes down like a blanket and envelops both me and the patient. On occasions I momentarily get a flash of orange in the centre of the green, and then I know it is the Buddhist monk working with me, as he gives me a glimpse of his orange robes. It is these guides who act as a go-between for us and the Spirit World, and it is through them that spirits work with us.

I should also state before moving on that there is absolutely nothing to fear in becoming a healer or a medium. I mention this simply because, there are some people out there who tend to get mediumship and spirit healing mixed up with those who dabble in the paranormal. The spirits we work with are our own loved ones who are now living a life on the other side, and who use their skill and talents to link with us. The paranormal are earthbound ghosts, whom you need to go looking for in haunted buildings etc. or by using a Ouija board.

The only discomfort I have ever experienced in the years I have been healing has been caused by an over-enthusiastic healing learner on the other side, who, like the healing learners on this side, have to start somewhere. On two occasions over the years, I have found myself linked with a healing spirit on the other side who was just learning the trade, so to speak. The healing energy he or she was channelling to me and through me to the patient was far too fierce. I suddenly found myself getting hotter and hotter, until I felt as though I were cooking from the inside out, and perspiration was literally running off me.

If you put four hundred amps through a piece of wire meant to take two hundred and fifty amps, it becomes overheated. We tend to do the same. We have our own temperature which should be comfortably warm, and if the healer on the other side channels healing energy at a nice gentle pace, we remain that way. But on these two occasions both these learners went at it too strongly, and channelled too fiercely, so I overheated. The thing to do on such an occasion is simply break the link. On the first occasion I was about to break the link when the energy eased off. So I assume someone on the other side twigged what was happening and took control. The second time I did break the link. But it was just a little uncomfortable, nothing more. With absent healing no such problems arise, because we are not laying on hands.

25
MY PRAYER FOR YOU

In my prayer for you, I asked for things
You would not ask yourself.
I asked the Lord to bless you,
And grant you long life, and good health.

I asked him too, to guide your hand,
In everything you do.
And I prayed that you would know the love,
Of friends, both good, and true.

I asked he give you peace of mind,
And keep away the tears.
And let contentment travel with you,
As you journey through the years.

I prayed too for fulfilment,
For joy in all you do.
And if in doubt which road to take,
I asked the Lord to lead you through.

And if, through age and memory lapse,
You should forget him too,
I asked that; in his goodness,
He will remember you.

And although my plea was not for gold,
When sending forth my prayer,
If the good Lord grants you all I ask,
You will be rich, beyond compare!

Richard John Scarr

26
ASBESTOSIS

Whatever kind of healer you might choose to become, healing works! For quite apart from the successes I have witnessed over the years, I too am living proof that it does work! I survived one of the ghastliest of lung diseases without any medical treatment whatsoever!

I had been experiencing breathing problems for quite a while before my wife passed, and then some two years on, when I was in my mid-seventies, my breathing became really bad. I had been a smoker since I was ten years of age, and it was only when I got to sixty-four that I finally managed to stop after many, many attempts. I was now in my mid-seventies. I had put my breathing problems down to the smokers' disease, emphysema. But finally, I decided to consult my doctor.

In order to reach his surgery, one had to climb a flight of stairs. By the time I walked into the room I was out of breath to the point I could not speak, but sat trying to get oxygen back into my lungs. My doctor asked how long I had been having breathing problems, and I told him some four years or so. He said he would arrange an X-ray and a visit to the cardiologist just in case it was my heart that was causing my breathing problem. In due course I had the X-ray, and a week or so later I got a call from my doctor to say, although it showed no evidence of cancer, there was suspect scar tissue covering one side of my right lung, and he wasn't sure what the cause of it was. He said he would arrange for me to see a specialist to have it investigated. In the meantime, I attended the cardiology clinic and had various tests.

After the tests I went back to see the heart consultant, who began by telling me that the tests on my heart showed no disease, although my heartbeat was a little slow. There was some furring of the arteries, but not excessive for my age. And then he threw me a googly! He asked, "How long ago is it since you came into contact with asbestos?"

That question took me aback. For the fact is, I had worked with powdered asbestos when I was a young man just after World War Two, and of course in those days it was not realised just what a dangerous material it really was. But I did not need the roof to fall in on me to appreciate he was now talking asbestosis of the lung!

Asbestosis grows over and into the lung. It was explained to me that it is a living spore that smothers and suffocates the lung, rendering it unusable, and it usually turns to cancer. But there is no treatment or cure for it.

The consultant then went on to say, "You have a large asbestosis scar on your right lung." Unlike my own doctor, he had recognised it for what it was. But then I suppose he saw a lot more of it among his patients than my own doctor did. Then he said, "Although I could be wrong, the disease doesn't appear be active at the present time." He then said, "I will write to your doctor and suggest he make an appointment for you to see a respiratory consultant," which of course, my doctor had already done.

As you can imagine, I had a lot to think about on my way home. It was over sixty years since I had worked with asbestos, and the asbestos spores had lain dormant all this time. And now, in my seventies, they had decided to make themselves known. So the wait to see a respiratory specialist was a worrying time, for I was now anxious to know — did I have asbestosis? Or had I had asbestosis? Had I just been handed a so-called death sentence, or a reprieve? It was not so much the going that concerned me as to the way I would go if I still had asbestosis.

Asbestosis, as with any cancer, is deadly. My brother-in-law, Bill, who had been a dock worker, and had also been exposed to asbestos, had developed the disease and eventually he succumbed to it, as did a neighbour of mine, who a few years previously had told me he had just been diagnosed with asbestosis. He passed over a little more than two years later. I now realised that at the time he was diagnosed, I too was suffering from the disease, which at that point would also have been active.

A week or so later, I kept an appointment with a consultant who was an authority on asbestos. A professor. After studying the X-ray, he shook his head then he turned to me and said, "You are a bit of an enigma, Mr Scarr. I don't know what you are doing. But whatever it is, keep doing it, for it is doing you good," and he then went on to explain that the asbestosis had spread down the side of my right lung, but it had not entered the lung. Nor was my left lung infected. The disease had simply cleared up, leaving scar tissue in its place. And although there was evidence of mild emphysema as a result of my years of smoking, the real cause of my breathlessness was due to the scar tissue on my right lung. Because scar tissue cannot expand, it had rendered my right lung pretty useless and had left me with breathing problems. But nevertheless, I was still here.

On reflection, I realised the disease would have been active too at about the time I took over as the new president of my church, and also as the new leader of the healing team. The previous healing leader had walked out — before the rest of the committee did so — and because she never returned, it fell to me to take over the running of the healing clinic. Over the years I had often received healing from my colleagues, and still do so on a weekly basis from a friend named Alan. When you give healing to someone, you receive healing as well, because some of that healing energy you are channelling to your patient stays with you. Hence my miraculous recovery from what should have taken me off. And although I have had several X-rays since seeing the consultant, nothing has changed in the last decade. Now, writing just a few weeks before my eighty-ninth birthday, there has been no reoccurrence of the disease.

27
SUCCESSES

Apart from my own, among some of the remarkable successes I have witnessed over the years, two in particular stand out in my mind. One of our patients, a lady, had been coming to the clinic for quite some time. She'd had colon cancer, for which she had been successfully operated on. Each time she came for healing she always went to the women members of our healing team. Then one week, when asked whom she would like to give her healing, she pointed to me and said, "I'd like to try the gentleman."

During the healing session, and as I was moving my hands down her back, one hand came to rest on a cold spot, and I asked her if she was suffering a back problem, to which she replied no. So I did not pursue the point. However, the very next time she came for healing she was tearful because she was suffering a great deal of pain in her back, and she had been to see her doctor, who had arranged a hospital scan for her. Then on her next visit to the clinic, she broke the news to us that the scan had revealed a tumour in her liver. So it was arranged that the lady should come for healing half an hour before the usual healing time, when all the healers would be free, and we could give her our undivided attention.

So on each healing morning the lady would arrive early, and while one of the healers laid on hands, the rest of us would sit around her in a circle sending her healing energy, and this went on for a number of weeks. The first sign that things were going well was when she said she was no longer in any pain.

Then on one of her visits she informed us she had received a letter from the hospital asking her to go for a scan with view to the surgeon performing an exploratory op. She attended the hospital and had the scan. But the following morning she received a phone call from the hospital asking her to go for another, because there seemed to be a problem with the previous one. And so she went for a second scan. The following morning the hospital consultant himself phoned her and asked if her ears had been burning, because she had been the topic of conversation among the staff at the hospital department. He told her the reason she had been asked to attend for a second scan was because they could not see the tumour on the first one, and thought it was faulty. But the second one also showed the tumour had completely disappeared from the scan.

That was some twelve years ago. The lady still comes for healing occasionally, and I'm pleased to say, is still doing fine.

***

The second incident happened after I had resigned from my own church. The phone rang the morning after my resignation, and the person on the other end was a lady named Mary, who had once been the healing leader at my church. But had quit, because like me, she could not tolerate the petty politics in the church at that time. She had moved on, and was now the healing leader at another church.

It was barely eight thirty a.m. when she rang, and although I had only given notice the previous evening, she was already aware of my resignation. So news travels fast, and she had rung to invite me to join her healing team at her new church, which I agreed to do.

Shortly after I had started healing at the new church, an elderly lady came into the clinic. As I was free at the time, having just finished giving a patient healing, she came to me. It was obvious to me that she wasn't in the least bit well. Her face was grey and haggard-looking, and she had dark rings under her eyes. I asked her if there was anything she would like to confide to me.

She was a little hesitant, and then she confided that she had just been diagnosed with cancer of the bladder, and she was in a great deal of pain. The cancer apparently was advanced enough for the consultant to be giving consideration to removing her bladder altogether. So, I gave her healing, to which she appeared to be quite susceptible. I felt her relax after a moment, her head lolled sideways in a state of drowsiness and it also took her a moment or two to come out of it when I had finished the healing.

The following week, Veronica, as I now knew her to be, again came for healing. I already had a patient in my chair when she entered the clinic. But I heard her ask Mary if she could wait until I was free, which was quite understandable. After all, if she went to another healer, she would have to go through the rigmarole of explaining her bladder cancer once again, whereas I already knew what was wrong with her. And so from then on, she made a point of coming to me every week, and if I already had a patient in my chair, she would wait.

Once again, the first sign of progress was when she said she was no longer in pain. Also, the dark rings disappeared from under her eyes and colour came back to her cheeks. Then, some weeks further on, she came in looking worried. She said she had received a letter from the hospital asking her to go for a scan, and so the fear that they might still decide to remove her bladder, a fear which had somewhat receded, now returned. But I reminded her of the fact that she was no longer in pain, and also that she certainly looked a lot better than when I had first seen her — so hopefully, the scan would show an improvement, and make surgery unnecessary.

The following week, on healing day, Mary unlocked the door and the first one into the clinic was Veronica. Instead of going straight to the desk to sign in, as she usually did, she stopped and looked in my direction and gave me a big smile. I knew she must have had good news. I took the smile to mean she had been told that surgery was no longer necessary.

When she finally sat down, she told me the scan had shown the cancer had reduced to little more than the size of a pea, which they finished off there and then with a laser. And so she had left the hospital in the knowledge that all future visits would be purely to ensure the cancer had not returned.

Because the healer is the only one the patient sees, and it is his or her hands the patient feels giving the healing, when relief or a cure, results from that healing, it is the healer the patient thanks. Sometimes out of pure relief, those thanks can be quite ardent; and this occasion was no exception. But when this happens to me, I have a stock-in-trade reply. I told her, "If I could heal you, Veronica, then I would be able to walk on water! But I cannot do either. So send your thanks to where they belong."

A few weeks later I left that church and returned to my own as its new president. That was ten years ago and I have not seen Veronica since. But I know she was still attending the clinic for healing some three years or so after I left that church, and was doing fine.

**

I have to say though, I have always been opposed to the term 'healer' being attributed to people like myself who lay on hands, and to that of absent healers. For the name healer gives the impression we ourselves carry out the healing. We do not! It gives the idea that we have a special gift. We do not! The healing comes from mightier hands than ours! The gift which we do have however, and which makes us extremely fortunate, is the privilege of being used as a channel — a tool through which those hands work! And the same privilege is open to each and every one of you. Once you begin to work for Spirit, whether as a clairvoyant, as a healer, or as a writer, producing writing that brings solace and comfort to those in need of upliftment, everything you do from then on will become spirit-inspired.

But the simple and undeniable truth is, no matter how well a medium performs, whether a platform or a healer, they are only as good as the spirit guide, and those in the Spirit World with whom they link. For it is those spirit beings who supply the evidence, and/or the healing energy with which the medium works. Just how well the medium gels with those they are working with on the other side depends entirely on the efforts and the dedication they themselves have put into their training, and the standard of awareness to which they have evolved. But no medium with a deep sense of the spiritual would claim to be anything other than what they are — an instrument, or a channel for the Spirit World with whom, and for whom they work!

28
THE HEALING HANDS OF GOD

I was sure the man who laid on hands,
Possessed a special gift.
For with the leaving of the pain,
I felt my spirits lift.

With great profuse, I thanked him,
My gratitude plain to see.
But he shook his head, and quietly said,
"The healing did not come from me."

"I am merely but a channel.
And the healing is not mine.
Nor can I walk on water!
Or change water into wine!"

"For like you, I too am mortal.
And to thank me would be wrong.
I am privileged just to be a tool.
So send your thanks to where they belong."

Then, on seeing light begin to dawn.
He said, and with a nod,
"My hands are just an instrument.
The healing hands are God's!"

Richard John Scarr

29
OTHER PLANES

There are said to be seven planes that make up the Spirit World, although I am not sure anyone knows for certain. But the Plane of Light is the one most inhabited. And why not? It is a wonderful plane where most people who have lived what are considered to be normal lives on Earth, mistakes and all, find themselves, and they are perfectly happy to remain there. Above the Plane of Light there are said to be four more that have come to be known as 'The Higher Planes'. Anyone who wishes to develop and seek more spiritual attainment can, after doing so, move up to a higher plane. The more spirituality you attain, the higher you can rise.

However, those of us who have lived selfish lives, by living solely for ourselves, with no thought for others, will spend time on what is known as the Grey Plane. This is a plane just below the Plane of Light. The Grey Plane is in part for those who have not really done anything bad in their lives, but have not really done anything good for others either, but have simply lived for themselves. It's a short stay, just to bring home to them how selfish they have been, and since they are not really bad people, they soon realise the error of their ways and repent, and are then reunited with their loved ones on the Plane of Light.

Yet we are expected to make mistakes while we are here, and in doing so, learn from them. Mistakes are part of the learning curve. For how else can we learn if we don't make mistakes? But there are those who constantly live their lives outside that of the learning curve — who steal and cheat other people for a living, and have absolutely no consideration for others, or even care whom they hurt. These too are bound for the Grey Plane until they are truly repentant; and no matter how competent they were at defrauding others on this side of life, repentance is something they cannot fabricate on the other side. So they only get to leave this plane when their repentance is genuine, and having lived a life of dishonesty, greed and selfishness off the backs of others, it can take time to find true repentance.

In the Summer Land, time means absolutely nothing. If you lost a loved one to Spirit ten years ago, although for you it might have been a long, lonely ten years, to the one who has passed it probably seems just like months. Often a medium will tell someone whom they are relaying a message to that the loved one they are linking with has not been over long, only to be told that they have in fact been over for a number of years. This is because, to the one in the Spirit World, time is completely irrelevant, and they truly feel they have only been over for a short time. This feeling is conveyed to the medium, thereby misleading him or her into believing that the one they are linking with really is new to the other side. In this context then, for those who end up on the Grey Plane, the time might not seem all that long. Or on the other hand, because time is irrelevant, I suppose it could also seem a great deal longer too.

For those people who have committed acts of out and out evil while on this Earth Plane, retribution does await. People who take the lives of others — murder and mutilate without compunction. Not only people like Hitler, Stalin, etc., and their faithful followers who kill without remorse, but all evil men and women who commit heinous crimes have to atone for them. There is a day of reckoning! Such people go to what Spiritualists call the Dark Plane, or Dark Zone, as some name it, and thank goodness for its existence. For it would be unthinkable if for instance, people like the Nazis who killed millions of men, women and children, herding them into the gas chambers to die, and sometimes even burning them alive, and who also killed in other unspeakable ways, were simply allowed to go unpunished. For the most part, I am sure that when people commit such horrendous crimes, it is without any thought for what might be waiting for them in the hereafter. Although I suspect that in their final moments, they somehow get an inkling as to what awaits them when they arrive on the other side — and it must terrify them.

What draws me to this conclusion is the number of haunted buildings where murder was committed, and the spirit of the murderer remains after his or her death. It could be they are simply too terrified to make their transition and face the consequences of their actions, and so they remain earthbound, and tied to the place where they committed their crime.

There is of course another possibility for the continued presence of the spirits of murderers etc. on the Earth Plane. It is possible that because they have become so evil and repugnant during their lifetime, none of their family members nor anyone else in the Spirit World wants anything to do with them, and so there is simply no one to take them over at the separation of their spirit and their physical being. And without someone from the other side to transport us, we remain earthbound.

People cannot hide behind excuses either. They cannot commit atrocities on the basis they were simply doing their duty as they saw it. Neither is it acceptable for someone to carry out some diabolical act of wickedness simply because they themselves would have been punished if they had not done so. Regardless of why we commit such heinous acts, we have to answer for them on the other side.

Political leaders who order the bombing and shelling of innocent civilians, while telling themselves what they are doing is justified and in the name of national security, and convince themselves they are merely protecting the lives of others, when in reality they are carrying out retaliatory revenge killings — they all go to the same place. The Dark Plane. For a murderer is a murderer. There is no justification for maiming or wanton killing, and so maliciously cutting short other people's life spans, even though it was their time.

Monsignor Robert Hugh Benson was a Catholic priest who, when he was on this Earth Plane, was a reluctant medium with the ability to link with the other side, and yet he had no understanding of Spiritualism. What he was experiencing went against all the teachings of the Catholic Church, and against what he himself actually believed and preached. As far as the Catholic Church was and is concerned, this sort of thing is the devil's work, and although he confided in colleagues, they were none the wiser either, and all they could do was to offer to pray for him. And so right up until the time of his passing, he was at conflict with himself and with the teachings of his religion.

When he made his transition, however, he was shocked and indignant to discover that all through the years of his priesthood he had been preaching some things that were simply not true, or were at the very best wide of the mark. He learned too, that the ability he had possessed while on the Earth Plane was not in fact the devil's work, but a wonderful gift. More than that, by being given the gift of being able to link with those who, now like himself, had passed to the Spirit World, he had in fact been given proof of life after death! And he was so disturbed by this discovery, and the fact that he had been preaching against what he now knew should be embraced and not demonised, he was determined to get the truth about life after death back to the Earth Plane in any way he could.

It was by linking with a medium named Anthony Borgia that he found a voice, and dictated what has since become something of an landmark text among books on the hereafter. It is called 'Life In The World Unseen' and it deals with the actual leaving of the spirit from the human shell at the moment of passing, and of its arrival in the Spirit World, and about life as is being lived by those on the other side. He also tells of being taken on a visit to a higher plane to meet a very important Egyptian, and of the kindness he was shown by those he met, who had evolved to higher planes. At one point he tells of being taken on a visit to the Dark Zone, which is situated below the Grey Plane, and is the very bottom plane. A place where not only do they live in perpetual darkness, and foul-smelling slime, but where not a bush or a tree exists — not even a blade of grass. The inhabitants arrive dressed in the clothes they usually wore on the Earth Plane, and which literally rot on their bodies. They not only live like animals, but their faces take on animal-like features also. And yet even they can eventually leave this foul place and move to the Plane of Light if they truly repent. But for some, it may take hundreds of Earth years.

30
THE LONGEST ROAD OF ALL

It is a long, long road to Heaven,
A hard climb to journey's end.
But it's a road that each of us must take,
Though fraught with twists and bends.

And adding to our burden,
Will be temptations on the way.
While the bends grow ever steeper,
Every time we go astray.

At times we will journey forward,
Just to find we are moving back.
Or going round in circles,
Because we have wandered off the track.

It is a lonely road to Heaven,
If we choose to walk alone.
But if we walk with Jesus Christ,
His steps will lead us home.

He will not smooth out our pathway,
For there are lessons to be learned.
But by walking at his elbow,
He will lead us through the turns.

It is a long, long road to Heaven,
But we can, with dogged stride,
Climb until we reach the top,
With the good Lord at our side!

Richard John Scarr

31
THE WAY SPIRIT WORK

At times Spirit works in wonderful and unbelievable ways, and at other times, in ways that mystify us Spiritualists also. I have witnessed and been on the receiving end of some remarkable incidents, one of which actually occurred while I was writing these pages.

Shortly after finishing the previous chapter, I was reading the manuscript over. When I had finished reading chapter nine, 'Nothing Spooky', and I was the reading the poem that I had originally followed it with, suddenly the title 'Follow My Directions' jumped into my mind. Not just as a passing thought, but quite vividly, as though I was suddenly remembering something very important. Now this was a totally different poem to the one I had already entered in the manuscript. It was in fact one I wrote some six or seven years earlier, and which I had quite forgotten about. I vaguely remembered it dealt with the position of the Summer Land to that of the Earth Plane, but I could not remember how the verses went. But it was obvious I was now being asked to replace the poem I had used with the poem 'Follow My Directions'.

I do not keep paperwork, it is too bulky. So I store everything digitally on CDs. So I patiently went through all the CDs I had burnt at that time, but the poem was not on any of them. A couple of CDs would not open, so it might possibly have been on one of those. Either way, I did not have a copy of the poem. At the time I wrote it, I was writing for just one website, although after a week or so my work would appear on others also. But the site I was writing for at the time, and which would have had a copy, had ceased to be with the retirement of the site owner. Nevertheless, I decided to search for it on the internet just in case one of the other websites had it. But nothing came up, which was not surprising really, in view of the time lapse. So I had to concede the poem was lost forever, and I had no choice other than to leave things as they were, and go with the poem I had already used.

Some four or five days later I switched on my PC to check my emails, and found one from the funeral website 'Creative Funeral Ideas' which is based in Canada. I had begun to send my poems to this site just before the other site owner retired and his website went offline. The email I had received thanked me for the poem I had supposedly recently sent them, and informed me that the poem was now up and running on their website, which was something of a surprise, in view of the fact I had not sent them any of my work for a number of months. I had sent them a couple of poems earlier in the year, but they had been written several years before. I had been busy with these pages, and had not been given anything in the way of a new poem. So I assumed the email was a mistake on their part. But when I opened the attachment, there on their website among the new articles they had just received was my lost poem, 'Follow My Directions'.

According to 'Creative Funeral Ideas', I had sent them the poem on 14th August 2017, for which they had then thanked me. They had then returned the poem to me by way of the attachment to their website.

As God is my witness, that poem did not come from me! I did not have the poem to send them! It was completely lost to me. Yet by clicking on the attachment, I now had a copy of it in my emails. When I read it and was able to refresh my memory of the poem, I realised just how much it resonated with the chapter 'Nothing Spooky' and it was, without any doubt, the ideal poem with which to follow it up, which of course explained why the Spirit World were not just keen for me to use it, they were determined by hook or by crook that it would be used. And that was their way of getting the poem to me. So I was able to replace the poem I had used with 'Follow My Directions'. But this is just one instance of how the Spirit World works with you, when you work for the Spirit World.

***

Our loved ones on the other side are not ghosts. They are living beings, and the very last thing they would want to do is to frighten anyone on this side. So, they are very careful in their dealings with their loved ones so as not to scare them. They are usually content to simply be around them and do their best to help when the need arises. But when we start to show an interest in the Spiritualist movement, and attend clairvoyance meetings, then believe me, there is no one more delighted than our loved ones on the other side of life. For one thing, it gives them the opportunity to make contact with us through a medium. And the more we become involved with Spiritualism, and the more aware we become, the closer they can draw to us, and the more they can interact with us. That is something they would never try to do if we did not have that awareness. There comes a time when we reach the stage when we are looking forward to our loved ones interacting with us, and doing things like tilting pictures on the wall, or moving articles out of place, or for instance, when saying good night to them, the phone goes 'peep peep' or its red light flashes. I have experienced all of these things.

On one occasion a nephew and his wife were visiting me, and seeing a photograph of my grandmother, his great grandmother, hanging on the wall, which was taken when she was only sixteen or seventeen years of age, my nephew asked who it was. My grandmother passed over when my mother was little more than a baby, so my mother had been raised by her own grandmother. My nephew had never seen the picture before. Having heard who it was, he walked over and stood looking up at it, and as he did so, the photograph jumped off the wall and he reached out and caught it as it dropped.

His face was a picture in itself to see. I explained to him that it was just his great grandmother saying hello, and letting him know she was around. After all, he had never seen a picture of her before, and was literally being introduced to her for the first time. Grandmother was not going to let a moment like that pass without commemorating it in some way or the other. A week or so later she, accompanied by my elder brother, who is the father of my nephew, came through to me via a medium and verified almost word for word what I had told my nephew. Grandmother had indeed been saying hello and letting us all know she was with us, which in itself was not scary for him. But it certainly gave him food for thought. I, on the other hand, thoroughly enjoyed the incident.

***

Some three years after my wife made her transition, she told me through a medium, "Be careful of the doorstep; it is dangerous."

At the time, painters had been working on the outside of the small block of flats in which I live. As I had not seen them for a couple of days, I assumed they were finished.

It was October, and rather late in the year for outside painting because of dampness. So when my wife warned me of the danger of a doorstep, of which both front and back are mahogany, I assumed they had been treated with weather proofing and that they were still wet. When I got home, I touched the front doorstep and it was bone dry. I then went through to take a look at the rear doorstep, and when I opened the rear door, I discovered neither the door nor doorframe had been painted. It soon became apparent as to why it had been left. The painters had dug away the rotting wood that held the step to the frame, and as a result, the step was now almost completely free of the frame and was merely balancing on some inch and a half of brickwork, beneath which there was a six-inch drop. Had anyone placed their weight on the step, it would have undoubtedly collapsed, and the result at best could have been a sprained ankle. The fact that I, or some other occupant of the building had not had an accident was pure luck, for the painters had not bothered to knock and warn any of us of the danger. At that time all the residents were elderly; I was able to alert them to this hazard.

Three days later I received a call from the contractor, who said, "You have probably noticed we have not painted the rear door or frame. They need to be replaced, and we will be back to do it next week." I was very tempted to tell him, actually, I am aware of it. But only because my wife did what your painters should have done! She warned me of the danger! Even though she passed over three years ago. But then I imagined him covering the mouthpiece of the phone with his hand, and turning to someone, and saying, "I've got a right one here!"

So I contented myself with the reply, "Yes, I am aware of it," and let it go at that.

**

One incident that happened in October 2007 still amazes me each time I think of it. As I mentioned at the beginning of these pages, my wife lost two babies to Spirit, neither of whom saw the light of day. In 2007 I began to get messages reminding me I had a boy in Spirit who had not set foot on the Earth Plane. Then in September of 2007 I received a message from the platform informing me my son had in fact been named David when he had arrived in Spirit, and I immediately assumed he had been named after one of my nephews, my sister's son who is also named David. This was later to be confirmed from Spirit.

Now as far as I was concerned, at that time my wife had four sons with her in Spirit, and whilst three were my stepsons, the fourth was our son, hers and mine. But I was not aware at that point of having a daughter in Spirit, simply because, as I now know, my wife had not been aware she was pregnant at the time. I was not to learn of the presence of a daughter in the Spirit World until December of 2016. This came as a huge, but pleasant surprise. By this time, had she been born, she would have been around forty years of age. However, as it turned out, there was a reason for my not being made aware of her presence until some forty years after her entry into the Summer Land, which I will explain later.

In September 2007, during a committee meeting, we decided we would hold a psychic supper at the church. This is an evening when church members get together for a meal, coffee and dessert. Seated at each table is a medium, and so everyone gets a ten or twelve-minute reading after the meal. It was decided the psychic supper would be held on November 17th, which was some seven or eight weeks away.

When I got home that evening, I decided to jot the date of the supper on the calendar, and taking the calendar off the wall, I turned the pages forward to November. As I did so, I literally stood rooted to the ground, for entered in my handwriting on the sixteenth of the month was 'David's Birthday', which I had no memory of having written.

I sat down at the kitchen table completely flummoxed, for there was no doubt about the fact that the handwriting was mine, and yet I could not remember having written those words. I must have sat there staring at that calendar for a good ten minutes.

Then I decided to check the old calendars, which I had kept since losing my wife in 2004, and which were stored in a kitchen cupboard. There was nothing entered in either the 2006 or the 2005 calendars, but when I turned to the November page of the 2004 calendar, there entered under the sixteenth were the words 'David. My Son's Birthday' and as I read those words it triggered something in my subconscious. At that moment I had a memory of myself leaning over the kitchen table in complete darkness, and I was writing something, but at the same time I was asking, "How can we be sure this is his birthday? We have only just been told his name!" But whoever I was contradicting was not answering me, much to my annoyance. But still I went on writing, even though I was irritated by the fact that my question was being ignored.

As this memory came back to me, I realised I had indeed written that entry. And not only that, I realised I had written it as though under protest. But the memory of doing so had been completely wiped from my mind. It was only when I read the words 'David. My Son's Birthday' that the memory was triggered, and then no doubt, only because I had become cross while writing it. However, I have absolutely no recollection of taking the current calendar from the wall and making the entry, 'David's Birthday'. That is still a complete blank.

I phoned a friend, who was also a very well-known and respected Brighton medium, Betty Horne. Betty, a lovely lady, had also been the president of my church for some twenty years or so. She had in fact been the president when I first joined the church. After telling her of the entries on the calendars and of the triggered memory, she told me I was a very lucky man, for I had experienced for myself, and had been given the proof that we really are two beings. A spirit in a physical frame.

Those in Spirit had again interacted with me. I had actually been brought from my bed while in sleep state. I had then gone into the living room where the pens are kept, after which I had then gone into the kitchen. Although I cannot be sure of the sequence, I had taken the calendar from the wall and turned the page to November and had then made the entry on the sixteenth, 'David's Birthday'. I had also taken the old calendars from a cupboard, and having found the one for 2004, I had made the entry, 'David. My Son's Birthday' and I now realise that it was the human side of me that was questioning the validity of the birthday date with the spirit side of me. My spirit side would have known of course that the date was correct, for my Spirit side spends time with those in the Summer Land.

All of this had, of course, taken place in complete darkness. But daylight and darkness are one and the same to Spirit, and since my spirit was in charge of what was taking place, I would have had no problems in writing in the dark.

After making those entries I had returned everything to its rightful place and then returned to my bed. When I awoke the following morning, I had no memory of what had occurred. And neither would I have ever remembered, and would have been left completely in the dark (no pun intended) as to those entries, if it had not been for the fact that the physical side of me had become annoyed, and so those written words had triggered my memory.

At first, I was puzzled as to why those two calendars were the only ones to be selected for those entries, and none of the others. Then the answer dawned on me.

2004 was the year his mother went over to join him in the Spirit World. So that was a very important year for David. So was 2007. For this was the year in which not only had I been reminded I had a son of my own in the Spirit World, but I had also been told the name given to him on the other side, and the date of his birthday. So this would be the first year I would be remembering and commemorating it with a card and flowers.

On 16th November 2007, I wrote the very first birthday card to my son David and placed it on the mantelshelf. I also bought mixed roses and took them to the church and placed them in a vase on the platform, and I know he was present while I was doing so.

The following evening, the seventeenth, I was back in the church for our psychic supper. After the meal the medium who was with us at our table began to give readings, and when it came to my turn, her first words were, "I have got to give you the name of David!" She then went on, "I don't know if this will make sense to you. But I have to give you what they are giving me. And they are saying on the other side, 'This one is yours! He is yours'!"

I knew what they were talking about of course. The other three boys who were with my wife were my stepsons. But David was ours. My wife's and mine. The medium then went on. "There was a celebration in the Spirit World very recently," and I told her it was David's birthday the previous day.

My son then made reference to the roses, and his first birthday card, and he was very moved to have received them. It was then that he made the comments I mentioned at the beginning of these pages. He said, "I'm fine, Dad. But I had to come back because I still had a lot to do on this side. *But I got what I came for!"*

As I mentioned earlier, my son David was named in the Spirit World after my nephew David, the son of my sister Doris and her late husband, Harry. He never saw the light of day; and so, the day he arrived in Spirit, which was the sixteenth of November, became his birthday. And just before midnight on 16th

November 2017, I received a phone call from my nephew, David, to say my sister Doris had passed over earlier that evening.

32
A TEAR AND A LOVELY ROSE

Thank you for the lovely rose,
You placed within my hand.
It is still as fresh and fragrant,
And blooming in the Summer Land.

I heard your tearful whisper,
As you said your last goodbye.
You whispered, "I will always love you!
And I will see you on the other side."

I knew your heart was breaking,
And how I wished we could embrace.
And then you bent to kiss me,
And a tear fell on my face.

And with that tear, I travelled on,
The rose held in my hand.
And with these tokens of your love,
I arrived here in the Summer Land.

And so, to keep me company,
What more could I have chosen?
Than wonderful memories of you,
A tear, and a lovely rose.

Richard John Scarr

33
A DAUGHTER IN SPIRIT

I first became aware of having a daughter in Spirit from a message from the platform. The medium, who was a very good friend of mine, said, "I know you have four boys in Spirit, Richard. But do you have a daughter in Spirit also?" and I told him I had not. He then shook his head and said, "Perhaps I am getting a crossed line," and he made no further reference to it.

Most Thursdays I go to a friend's house to have healing. My friend Alan is the son of the late renowned Brighton healer, Tom Pilgrim. Alan is also a healer and a medium. This particular Thursday was just a week after the reference had been made from the platform about me having a daughter in Spirit. Alan was about to lay his hands on my shoulders, when he broke off, and he said, "I have your wife here. And she is saying she has your daughter with her!" But I shook my head, and told him I didn't have a daughter in Spirit. But he insisted, "I can't take it away. Your wife says she has your daughter with her!"

It was at that point I remembered the reference I had received from the platform the previous week, about a daughter in Spirit, and I told Alan about it.

He then said, "Your wife didn't even know she was pregnant at the time. And neither did she know of your daughter's presence in the Spirit World until very recently, because your daughter was taken to a higher plane within weeks of arriving in Spirit. And none of your relatives on that side knew of her existence either. But she has now been released back to the Plane of Light, and into the bosom of her family on that side." He then added, "Your daughter is here also. But because she has never communicated, she has to learn to how to do so. But she will be coming through to you once she has learned how."

Every night when I go to bed, my wife and I have a chat for half an hour or so, and needless to say, I had some questions to ask her on this particular night. My first question was about my daughter's name, and I got, "Latricia." I also asked her birthday, which of course meant the day of her arrival in Spirit, and I was told, "The sixth of July." And I also got, "Be patient." I took this to mean my daughter would communicate when she had learned how.

On the last Saturday of each month, the public can walk into our church and get a private reading between the hours of twelve noon and four p.m. without having to book it first. There are always two mediums on duty, and one of them is usually Louise Eaton, our president.

When I stepped down from the presidency of my church just after my eightieth birthday, I had handed it over to my vice president. However, she was not willing to take on the job as president unless I agreed to stay on as vice president for at least a year to help her cope. And now, eight years later, it has been something of a long year. When, some four years after taking on the job, the serving president decided to resign due to personal reasons, and although I was still the serving vice president, I was reluctant to step back into the top job.

Louise Eaton, our new president, is blind, and has been since childhood. Louise is also a brilliant medium. I have had the privilege of working with some very good mediums over the years, and Louise is one of the best, probably the best I have ever worked with! She is without doubt the best in Brighton. The Spirit World compensates her for her disability by giving her astounding evidence during her work on and off the platform. For instance, if you were present at someone's passing, she will tell you which side of the bed you were sitting on. She will also give you the date, the day and time of that passing. If you visited that person in the chapel of rest and placed something in the casket, she will tell you what it was you placed there. If it was a card, she will tell you what you wrote on it. Such is her evidence. She has a huge following, both in Brighton and beyond. Her name should be up there among the best! And the following pages will demonstrate just how closely the Spirit World works with her.

On one occasion after having had healing at Alan's home, he asked me to hold out my hand. He then went through the motions as though placing something in my hand, and then folded my fingers closed. He then told me I had symbolically been given a feather from the Indian healer, Grey Wolf.

Grey Wolf was a famous North American Indian healer, long since passed over. He is also Alan's guide. Why he had given me this feather, albeit symbolically, neither Alan nor I had any idea!

I had accepted that feather in the spirit in which it had been given; and when I arrived home, I symbolically placed it within my wife's photo frame, saying, "I am leaving this feather in your care, Bell."

That evening I was down to chair for the medium who was due to preside over an evening of clairvoyance at the church. But the weather was really miserable, chucking it down with rain, and only six people turned up. And so, instead of an evening of clairvoyance, the medium decided to hold a little experimental circle, in which everyone would get a message anyway.

Having set the chairs in a circle, the medium asked us to place our clenched hands on our knees, close our eyes and relax. She then asked the Spirit World to symbolically give each of us a present. We sat silently like this for some ten minutes. Then the medium brought us back, and asked each one in turn what they had been given.

Everyone in that circle, except me, said they had been given a feather!

I then realised why I had symbolically been given that feather by Grey Wolf that afternoon. I was meant to bring to the church in the evening. He had known it would be needed. I had started to explain this to those in the circle, when the lady sitting on my left said, "Your wife is standing between us!" and then it all fell into place! And I knew why my wife was there.

I had, of course, failed to do what I was supposed to do. I had symbolically placed that feather in my wife's photo frame, and there I had left it. I had not retrieved it before coming to the church, and so my wife, bless her, had brought it to the church for me.

Then, about a year later, again after receiving healing, Alan reached across and made as though he was attaching something to my lapel. He then said, "You have just been symbolically presented with a medal by the Spirit World." I looked at him a little questioningly, and he said, "They are saying 'It is for service'."

So, as with the feather, once again I accepted that medal in the spirit in which it was given, and when I arrived home, I again did what I had previously done. I symbolically placed it within my wife's photo frame for safe keeping, and I forgot all about it, and the feather.

That was quite some time ago. Then one evening recently I was sitting in the congregation, and Louise was the clairvoyant on the platform. She threw out some information that resonated with me, and I knew she had my wife with her. I let her know I could take the information, and then she said, "I am in your living room and I can see your wife's photo frame hanging close to some flowers."

This was spot on! My wife's photo does indeed hang beside a small corner shelf on which there is a vase of artificial roses etc. And she then went on. "There are three items contained within the frame with her photo."

Although I never like to tell a medium he or she has got it wrong, there is no point to letting them believe something is right if they have made a mistake, and so I told Louise, "Actually, there is only one thing in the frame with my wife's photo. And that is a lock of her hair!"

She came back immediately with, "What about the feather?"

That just struck me dumb for a moment, and before I could say another word, Louise went on. "And there is also something silver and shiny tucked inside the frame. It looks like a piece of jewellery." I knew immediately what she was seeing. I told her it was in fact, a medal!

That then, is the calibre of this lady's gift! There is in fact only one item of substance in that frame with her photograph, and that is a lock of my wife's hair. Both the feather and the medal had been given to me symbolically, in spirit form, and had been placed in the photo frame in the same way. And yet, Louise could see all three items!

When the vacancy for president arose, the question of Louise taking on the job was suggested by the outgoing president, and it seemed that Louise was keen to accept the position. She was a member of our church and a member of the committee at the time, and she is now also a member of our healing team. Although there would be some things she would not be able to do, because of her disability, such as the signing of cheques etc. I and the other members of the committee felt it would be unfair to let this stand in the way of her taking on the job if she wanted to do it.

In accord, she was voted in as our new president. And a very good one she turned out to be! She gives a great deal of herself to the job. I remained vice president for the next couple of years, until I was finally able to hand it over to someone else. Though I am still a committee member at the time of writing, and still healing.

So, having been made aware of a daughter in the Spirit World, and having ascertained for myself her name etc. I decided I would go along to the church on the Saturday, which was the day of the drop-in readings, and have a reading with Louise. I actually arrived at the church about ten minutes or so before she did. When she walked in and I made my presence known, she said, "I knew you were going to be here today, Richard. I received word from the other side to say you would be."

During the reading, in which Louise gave me a great deal of good evidence, she got on to the subject of my daughter, and she said, "Richard, your daughter is so spiritual, I feel almost privileged to be talking to her. But I am having problems with communication. She is only using small and simple words. And it is almost as though she is only just learning to speak. But she is saying give her time, and she will come through to you." She added, "Your daughter is not used to communicating by word of mouth, but by thought only," which presumably is the way they communicate on the higher planes.

I then asked Louise the name given to my daughter in Spirit. I wanted to verify that what I had been given was correct. She said, "She has two names. When she first went over she was given the name Latricia. But she was renamed Angela on the higher plane. But she says you can call her by either name." I then asked her to verify Angela's birthday, and after a moment, Louise replied, "The seventh of July." But I was sure I had heard the sixth of July, which of course meant one of us had misheard. But it was important that I get it right. For from this moment on I would be commemorating the day with flowers and a card. So I asked her to reaffirm the date, and this time Louise replied, "Sorry, it is the sixth of July, not the seventh."

The following Thursday I was back at Alan's home, and there was quite a number of people from the other side present, which included my wife and Alan's wife, Anne (he also is a widower), my daughter, Angela and my mother, among many others. There was a huge party spirit, and Angela was over the moon with elation. She said she had been embraced by both sides of the family, my wife's and mine. Brothers, sisters, cousins, aunts, uncles, grand and great grand folk going back to who knows when. I can imagine her feelings, having spent all those years on the higher plane since being a baby, without any close family. I treasure her words, made just before Alan broke the link to begin the healing session. She said, "I am mastering it, Daddy!" which meant of course that she was learning to communicate.

The weeks went on and I waited for a message from Angela. Although she was present with my wife and often other members of my family at Alan's home, no message was forthcoming. However, she is also present with my wife every night to say good night, and I clearly hear her say, "Goodnight, Daddy, I love you." But there were still no 'one to one' messages. July came, and her birthday. I bought a birthday card and a nice bunch of flowers which I took to the church. Then, almost two weeks later, while in bed and at that drowsy stage, I got, "Go for a reading!"

So on drop-in Saturday I went to the church and again had a reading with Louise. And although my wife let me know she was present, she took a back seat so to speak, and Angela stepped forward and began a 'one to one' with me, and she had certainly learned how to communicate, bless her heart. For the next half an hour, no one else on that side got a look in, and no one interrupted her but left her with a clear field. She thanked me for the flowers on her birthday, and said she loved her birthday card. It was her first one ever, and she said she liked the butterflies that were on the front of the card, which I had forgotten about. She then said that she had guided me to that card and got me to select it. My wife is always with me when I go shopping, and this time of course, Angela was with her. I did in fact pick up the card, and then replace it on the shelf and looked at others. But then I went back to the original one and selected that. Now I know why. And so has begun what I hope is the beginning of many more 'one to one' messages with my daughter, along with my other loved ones.

But this was not the first time a medium had been told from the Spirit World that I would be at a certain place at a given time. It had happened once before. The medium who had first made reference from the platform to my having a daughter in Spirit is a very good friend. His name is Francis, another renowned medium, from Kent, also with a good following.

On one occasion he was due to take to the platform for an afternoon of clairvoyance at a Spiritualist church in Hove. Unbeknown to him, I decided to attend the church myself that afternoon and take him several new poems I had recently finished. He is one of several mediums who use them from the platform.

Again, I arrived at the church before him, and when he walked in, he didn't seem in the least surprised to see me. We shook hands and I handed him the new poems. When he took to the platform, it was for an afternoon of very good clairvoyance and evidence, and then he told the congregation that before he had left home that day, he had selected one of my poems which he had intended to read as a finish to the afternoon. Once on the train, he reached for the poem in his pocket only to discover he had left it at home. He then said, "Now what am I going to do, Spirit?" He told us, "And at that moment, in my mind's eye they showed me an image of Richard Scarr, and he was holding something white in his hand. And so I knew he would be here at the church with some poems. And sure enough, when I walked in, there he was. And he placed some new poems in my hand!" And that of course explained why he had not been surprised to see me, and he finished off the afternoon by reading one of the new poems.

34
MUM

Lord, you knew what you were doing,
When you made our mum!
You knew you had reached perfection,
And could never make another one.

You had made a one-off model,
So you threw away the mould.
You gave Mum the patience of a saint!
And a heart of pure gold!

You gave her eyes that never looked
For fault in anyone.
You filled her soul with so much love,
And compassion by the ton.

You gave her sympathetic ears,
And such understanding too.
She would always lend a helping hand,
If there was something she could do.

Friends come in many guises,
But there was no friend like Mum.
Lord, you must have felt so proud,
When you saw what you had done!

To some, she may have seemed naïve,
But those who love her, knew her worth.
For Lord, when you created Mum,
You placed an angel on this Earth!

Richard John Scarr

35
JANINE

One Thursday, and just as Alan laid his hands on my shoulders to begin the healing, he broke off again, and he said, "Two of your brothers are here with your wife, Bell, and your daughter, Angela. And there is also a young girl with them, about ten years of age. And as they came in, the child ran straight over to you, and she looked really pleased to see you. And it was quite obvious that she knows you well."

I was somewhat puzzled by this piece of information, for there had been no loss of a child of this age in my family.

Then after a moment, he said, "She is being fostered! She is living with your family on the other side. Bell has been asked to take care of her. So no doubt that is how she comes to know you too. She knows you from when you visit in your sleep state."

Now this was complete news to me, for I had not been given an inkling concerning an addition to my family in the Spirit World. Because we are not allowed to bring memories of our visits back with us, I had no knowledge of this young girl whatsoever. And so again, I had some questions to ask Bell that night, and the first one was the child's name. I was given 'Janine' and I was told she was eleven years of age. But when I asked why she was being fostered, I sensed a reluctance to say why. I then asked her birthday; I was given the fifteenth of February. From that moment, every night, when saying my good nights to my family in Spirit, I always included Janine, and she always replied with, "Good night, Uncle."

When her birthday came round I bought her a pretty birthday card. But instead of buying her flowers, I bought her a cuddly stuffed toy, a dog. For I knew that our loved ones have the ability of being able to reproduce these things in Spirit. So I knew she would have both the card and the cuddly toy with her on the other side.

Then, while having a reading with Louise one morning, the subject of Janine's fostering arose and I asked her if she could glean any further information, for the information I had was sketchy to say the least. After a moment, she told me that they were still reluctant to say very much on the other side, other than that Janine had been treated very badly on this side before going over.

Now, I didn't know if it was this bad treatment that was responsible for her transition. But if her parents had been part of her ill-treatment, then they would never again be allowed contact with her on the other side.

For the next twelve months or so I said good night to her as part of my family, and always got a, "Good night, Uncle." Then one night, having said good night to her, and although I wasn't certain, I thought heard her say, "Good night, Dad!" So the next night, when saying good night to her, I listened intently, and sure enough, when I said good night to Janine, I heard her say, "Good night, Dad!"

As a result, I was in no doubt that she had been made a permanent part of our family. I asked my wife if this was the case, and I was immediately treated to the cobweb feeling. "Yes!"

Since then, I have noted Janine has changed "Good night, Dad," to "Good night, Daddy!" and I can only assume this is because she and Angela come in together to say good night. Angela always says, "Good night, Daddy," and so this is probably why Janine has changed her good nights too.

It was something like two months after Janine's fostering had become a permanent adoption, and my knowledge of the full facts was still sketchy. I woke one morning in the early hours, and squinted at the clock on my bedside table, and if I remember rightly, it was a little before two o'clock. I then I turned over and settled down to sleep again. But instead of dropping straight off again as I usually did, thoughts of Janine came into my mind. And then, before I could prevent it, all sleep had left me and I was wide awake with thought after thought of her flooding into my mind. It took several minutes before it dawned on me that they were not just random thoughts. I was actually being given an explanation as to how she came to be part of our family. And although the part about her treatment before she went over was still a blank, by the time I went back to sleep I was able to dot the 'i's and cross the 't's.

Exactly as in the case of Angela, when Janine went over, she had been taken to a higher plane almost immediately. She was little more than seven months old at the time. And there she had remained until she had turned eleven years of age, and without any contact with relatives of any kind.

Angela, of course, had by that time been on that plane for some thirty years, although she would in reality have looked little more than twenty-one or so. And she also had had no contact with relatives in all those years, for as I mentioned earlier, neither Bell nor anyone else on that side knew of her existence. But at some point during Janine's time on that plane, she and Angela became known to each other.

Although I am not completely sure when or how they became acquainted, I believe it was because Angela had something to do with Janine's education on that side. She works with children, and so Angela became like a big sister to Janine. When the decision was taken to return Angela to the bosom of her family on the Plane of Light, for Janine, it was literally like losing her only sibling. She missed and began to pine for Angela, so much so that finally the powers that be took the decision to return Janine also, and where better to place her than within the bosom of Angela's own family, where she and Angela would really become sisters, and who better to be her mother than my sweet and loving Bell?

I of course, only come into the equation when I go over in my sleep state, and won't be a full-time dad to her until I too make my transition. But nevertheless, as far as Janine is concerned, in her eyes, I am the man! And that is how Bell and I came to have two daughters in Spirit, when we hadn't even been aware we had one — and of course, with four boys in the family also, life on that side won't be dull. Now who says life does not go on in the Summer Land?

Just a month after Janine's birthday is the birthday of one of my great grandchildren, Rhonda. It is on the twelfth of March. She was to be two years old on the one coming up. Her sister, Saoirse, had already had her fourth birthday in the September. I was sitting one afternoon making conversation with my wife, and receiving really fierce energy in the way of the cobweb feeling, and I mentioned to her the fact that our great granddaughter's birthday was due soon. I said I would follow my usual practice, and give the money rather than shop for presents. Then her parents could buy her something. And it was at that moment I heard within my own mind, "Give her the doggie!"

For a moment I wondered if I had imagined it. I asked my Bell, "Did I really hear that? Did I just hear Janine tell me to give Rhonda her cuddly toy?"

I was instantly showered with energy. "Yes."

Janine, of course, would already have the doggie in replica with her on that side. So the cuddly toy sitting on display in my bedroom was surplus to requirements. But then it also occurred to me that Saoirse had already had her birthday, and it would not be fair to make fish of one and fowl of the other. The answer of course was to buy Janine another cuddly toy, so there would then be two toys coming from her — and this I did. I bought a cuddly pussy cat for her. So she now has two cuddly toys with her on the other side, and I had the same here. So, I was able to give one to each of our two great granddaughters, as a gift from Janine.

Of course, they were too young to understand the significance of their toys, or the fact that the idea had actually come from a young girl in the Summer Land, who was now related to them.

36
VISITORS

With all the clairvoyance and healing etc. that goes on, and has gone on for over a hundred years at our church, one would expect a few spirit beings to be in residence in the building. And yet in all the years I had been at the church I had never experienced anything out of the ordinary, although I am often alone there, as are other committee members also. Of course though, when we are present in the church, then naturally various members of our loved ones from Spirit are bound to be present. My wife is always at the church whenever I am, and often lets me know by giving me a gentle cobweb-like feeling on my face while I am healing. Just enough to make her presence felt.

On one particular Friday, I had arrived early and alone, and was setting things out ready for the healing clinic. Then Louise walked in, and she asked, "Have you got a son named Nigel in Spirit?" and I told her my eldest stepson was named Nigel. He had passed as a result of a drowning accident. She said, "As I was approaching the church door just now, a voice at my side said, 'I am Richard's son, Nigel'!"

It seemed, because I was present at the church, Nigel had decided to join us, although he never made his presence felt again after that initial introduction.

On another occasion I was speaking to another committee member about my sister, Vera, who has passed over, when Louise happened to walk in, and she asked, "Have you got a sister named Vera in Spirit?" I told her I had, and that I had just been talking about her. Louise replied, "She is here. And she was listening to every word you were saying."

Then, for some reason, we suddenly began to get other visitors too. One Friday Louise came from the loo into the kitchen, and she said, "As I left the loo just now, a woman's voice said, 'Hello'." And even as Louise was speaking, the name Marie popped into my mind. I knew immediately who had spoken to her. Marie had been one of our church members — a lovely lady who had been far from well. She had suffered from chronic asthma among other things, and regularly had very bad attacks which left her fighting for breath. She used to come for healing on Fridays. But very often she would turn up at the church on a Thursday or Sunday when we held services, and she would be in the throes of an attack. I would take her into the healing sanctuary and give her healing, and on each occasion the procedure was the same. She would be wheezing as she fought to get oxygen into her lungs, and I would start the healing process. After a moment I would feel her start to relax as the wheezing got less and less and her breathing improved, and she would then sag forward as she became drowsy. I would hold her head so that her chin could not fall forward onto her chest and so close the airways. When she finally came out of it, she would be sleepy, but the attack would have passed.

Then, she stopped coming to church, and some two or three months later, I was at a neighbouring church for an evening of clairvoyance. The medium came to me and said, "I have a lady named Marie here. And she wants to thank you for all the healing you gave her. And for the friendship she received at your church." And so, the lovely lady had passed over. About a week later we got word from her sister to say Marie's funeral was to take place the following week. So Marie must have come through to me almost immediately after passing. It seems that on this particular Friday, she had chosen to pay us a visit.

Then yet again on another Friday, one of our healers brought with him to the church a little machine that looked something like small recorder. Apparently, it was supposed to pick up and record spirit voices. So, accompanied by Louise and myself, he took the recorder into the church. Switching on the machine, he asked if anyone was present. Then on switching back to play, there came a very muffled and indistinguishable voice. On turning the machine back to record, Louise asked, "Is anyone here?"

A voice from down near the platform replied, "I'm Frank," and it sounded very gruff and irritable.

Louise remarked, "He doesn't sound all that pleased to be talking to us."

When she asked him who he was, he replied, "Go away!" and so we decided to do just that. As we were not using the church that day, we closed the door and left Frank to it. Whether he is resident or was just visiting, I don't know. And although quite frequently I am alone at the church, as are other members of the committee too, he had never made his presence known before.

About two weeks after this incident, we decided to check to see if Frank was still around. So Louise, Alan, who was another of our healing team and I went into the church. While Louise sat down near the platform where we had heard Frank's voice, Alan and I sat nearer the back. Immediately Louise and I smelled cigarette smoke as though someone was smoking in the church. Alan, being a smoker himself, could not smell it. Then Louise and I both had a clairsentience moment. We both felt 'cancer' and then Louise got 'fisherman'.

As far as I am aware, Brighton has never been a fishing port. But a few miles down the coast is Newhaven, and that was and is a fishing port, with a fishing fleet. So it looked as though our spirit had been a fisherman during his lifetime, and had passed over with cancer.

We sat there for several more minutes but picked up nothing more. So whoever had been present had either left, or no longer wanted to link with us. And although this person had not given his name, we assumed it was Frank.

37
IF I COULD VISIT

All my prayers lead up to Heaven.
And if I could use them as a mould,
I would shape them like a spiralling stairway,
And climb to Heaven's gates of gold.

And there I would knock and tell the angels,
How much I miss your lovely smile.
And how lonely I have been without you,
And could I visit for a while?

I would tell them it would mean the world,
If I could spend some time with you.
Just holding hands the way we used to,
And spend a pleasant hour or two.

If I could hold you for a moment,
And feel the comfort of your touch.
If I could have the chance to tell you,
I still love you very much!

If I could see your lovely face,
And gaze into your loving eyes.
I would return to Earth and never question
The hows or whys, of our goodbyes.

I would wait until I too could leave,
And cross 'The Great Divide.'
And those hours that I spend with you,
Would keep me till I am by your side.

Richard John Scarr

38
SPIRIT INSPIRED

I had been writing verse for a number of years. But they were ordinary-type poems as opposed to spiritual.

However, when my wife passed over, I stopped writing altogether. In fact, I practically stopped doing most things. Then one evening while at my church, a medium said, "I have your grandmother on your mother's side here. And she is asking, why you have stopped writing?"

Now quite honestly, that seemed a strange question to ask. For she of course knew that over the preceding twenty years or so my family had gradually dwindled until I was now living alone. Two of my stepsons had passed over, both in adulthood, and then my wife too passed, leaving myself and a third stepson who was wheelchair-bound, having some five years previously become paralysed from the chest down. He had his own wheelchair-friendly flat. It fell to me to visit, and do what I could to take care of him. Then just eighteen months after my wife passed — it was just before midnight on a Saturday — I received a phone call to say that he too had been found dead in his wheelchair.

I have an adopted son named Richard too, from my first marriage. But he was living in London at that time, and I was on my own. So I think, given my situation at that time, it was perfectly understandable why I was not in the mood for writing poems.

I think the problem is, although they don't mean to be unsympathetic, some of those in Spirit are apt to forget what grief is like on this side, especially those who have been in the Summer Land for a long time. My grandmother had been over since she was twenty-seven years of age, and my mother was little more than a baby of three or four (she was brought up by her own grandmother). My mother passed in her late eighties, and I am in my eighty-ninth year. So as you can see, my grandmother had been gone well over a hundred years, and yet it was 2007 before she decided to come through to me. By then I was seventy-six years of age, and even then, she came through to me only because I had looked at her photograph and asked if she was still on the other side. A week later she came through in answer to that enquiry, and apart from the incident when she caused her photograph to jump off the wall a few years later, she has only ever been through on three occasions in all.

She of course is living in a perfect environment herself and can visit our plane at the drop of a hat, as can all our loved ones on that side. Besides which, her nearest and dearest on this side, including myself, visit there quite frequently during our sleep state, and we spend time with her and our other loved ones. So understandably, because she sees us frequently, she, like a lot of the long-timers in the Spirit World, tend to forget that it is the spirit side of us that gets to see them during these trips over. And as a result they can become a bit complacent, because some of them tend to forget that it is the human side of us that does the grieving, and is also the part of us that feels lonely, because it does not have the same ability as that of our spirit side. It neither visits, nor has it the ability to see our loved ones when they are here with us from the other side.

I have three brothers in Spirit, and one of them, Harold, passed over when he was four years of age, before I was even born. And yet not once in all the years I have been a Spiritualist had he been through to me. Neither had I even heard his name mentioned by a medium. I had asked several times if he was still over there, hoping if he was, he would let me know. Then, on one occasion while receiving a message from other loved ones, I asked the medium if Harold was still around, and he came back immediately with, "Of course I'm still here! And you and I get along like a house on fire when you visit in your sleep."

Like Grandmother, he never thought it necessary to come through before, because he too sees his relatives from this side frequently when we go over during our sleep state. And of course, he too can visit whenever he wishes. He has not been through to me again since.

I honestly believe it is all down to what the long-timers became accustomed to, when they went over, and I am talking of people like my grandmother and my brother Harold who have been over some ninety-odd years, plus. Spiritualism then was still taboo for many people. There were few spiritual churches about. Even in the fifties and sixties for instance, when my mother and elder sister wanted to attend a Spiritualist meeting, I would take them to the Spiritualist main centre in Belgrade Square in London because there was nothing local. So the long-timers in Spirit had little chance of communicating with loved ones through a medium, and I believe they simply became accustomed to not communicating. Though of course, they would still spend time with us, and we with them. Now, even though there are opportunities for them to come through, I believe old habits die hard.

For those who have moved over during the past twenty-five years or so it is a different story. Spiritualist churches have sprung up in practically every town, and more and more people have turned to Spiritualism. So the newcomers to the Summer Land have been able to communicate with loved ones on this side almost from the day they went over, and they do so at every opportunity.

I have reminded those who have been over a long time on several occasions of their seeming reluctance to come through, pointing out that, although they and the spirit side of us get together often, it is the human side of us that needs to hear from them, because those messages bring us comfort and a feeling of closeness. When the long-timers become complacent in this manner, they are unwittingly neglecting the human side of their loved one on this side.

But getting back to my grandmother. She went on to say, "Get back to your writing and I will help you." So when I arrived home that evening I decide to put her offer to the test. I didn't use a computer in those days; I used a word processor, which was an advanced form of electric typewriter. I settled down with the processor and almost immediately I began to write, and before I went to bed that night, I had written a six-verse poem.

The following morning, I went back to the poem and did a bit of changing and polishing until I finally had the finished work, and the result of this collaboration between my grandmother and me can be found at the end of the chapter four It is titled 'Don't Grieve For Me'.

***

It seems, however, my poems have the ability to corrupt even the most godly of us. Some time ago I was approached by one of the lady members of our church for a copy of 'Don't Grieve For Me'. Her husband had just made his transition; she wanted the poem read at his funeral and I of course was happy to oblige. Then a few days after the funeral, she approached me again and asked if she could have another copy. It appears the service had been conducted by a local vicar, who had read out the poem as the lady had requested. But after the funeral the lady completely forgot to ask him to return it. However, when she phoned him the following morning and asked for the poem, he was reluctant to part with it. He told her that he wanted to keep it in order to use it at future funeral services, and he suggested she request another copy from me.

This has me wondering. When the time comes, and this poem-pinching reverend gentleman has to meet his maker, how will he justify his filching of the only copy of the poem this poor widow woman possessed? Fire and brimstone must surely await him!

After writing this poem, I began to write again on a regular basis. Then some seven or eight years ago I found myself writing nothing but spiritual poems, and gradually the volume of these grew until I was writing seven or eight hours a day for weeks on end. Some of these poems contained as many as twenty verses. In fact some of them were literally a story in verse. I would wake in the mornings with bits of verse rattling around in my brain, and usually a title repeating itself over and over again. I would sit down with my computer; the inspiration and theme were there in my head and before long a new poem would have taken shape. I would then spend some time completely changing verses and words until I was satisfied with it, and usually the finished poem rarely resembled the initial effort.

There were times too when I would actually wake in the night with bits of verse rattling in my brain, and I would have a job getting back to sleep. There have been times when I have given up trying, and then I would find myself writing sometimes before five in the morning. I would be so engrossed, I would forget all about breakfast. In fact I would forget about everything other than my writing, with the result that, before I knew it, it would be two or three in the afternoon and I would realise that I had not had a thing to eat.

Now I have to confess, there was a time when I thought these poems were all my doings, because I had been writing for many years, although not spiritually. But then one evening while being given a message from the platform, the medium said, "I have a lot of writing with you," and he then went on to say, "I'm sure you know that it is all spirit inspired! They want you to do just what you are doing. You are putting the word out there." And that of course explained why it was that I was continually waking with this stuff rattling around in my head.

Twice more I was told by mediums that my work was spirit inspired, and from that moment I stopped taking the credit. If anyone said to me, they liked such and such a poem, my reply was always, "It is not my doing. It came from the other side," and this went on for some time. Then on one occasion I was having a private reading, and the medium said, "They want me to tell you. You can take credit! They are saying, it is a collaboration between you and them. When they give you something, you have free will," and later, when I sat down to think about this, I realised this in fact was exactly the case.

The most important part of any writing is that first inspiration! The initial idea, the theme, or concept. One can sit for days or even weeks or months without getting the sniff of an idea. It is what professional writers call 'writer's block'. But I was getting that inspiration month in and month out. I have placed over eighty poems and prayers on the web in some ten years, and in that time, I think have only experienced a writer's block on one occasion, and it finally dawned on me just what they were doing.

They were giving me the most important part of any writing. The inspiration. The initial idea and concept. They were even giving me a working poem. Hence the lines rattling around in my head when I first awake. They are the verses I initially put on my computer, after which I am free to run with it, and change and shape it in any fashion I wish, or even discard and replace, as I often do, until I am satisfied that I have the finished article. Usually once completed, this has little resemblance to the one I have been given. And so, I now accept that it is a collaboration between them and me.

However, having said that, they will change something if they think they have a better line or verse to that which I have written. Several times I have placed a poem on the web, only to wake one morning days or weeks later to find that poem running through my mind, and a line or a complete verse has been changed. I end up placing that on the web too, with the changes, and in most cases I have had to admit their line or verse was better.

Nevertheless, I found myself losing a lot of sleep. For sometimes I would only have been asleep two or three hours when I would wake with something running through my brain, and then I would find it almost impossible to doze off again. So I asked Spirit to stop giving me this material at night, and to give it to me during the day instead, and bless them, that is exactly what they did. The problem was however, they chose some very awkward moments to interact with me. It was usually when I was watching and engrossed in something on television.

Twice I was watching a World Cup football match when bits of verse started forming in my brain, and so I had no choice but to switch off and get my computer out. On one occasion I was actually attending a funeral at a crematorium when it started. At home I simply have to switch off the television set. But I could not switch off the vicar who was taking the service, and so I had his voice droning in my ears while at the same time I was formulating a poem in my head, and also doing my best not to look as though my mind was wandering and I wasn't paying attention. But fortunately, the service was nearly over, and I left the crematorium with the first verse of a working poem already captured in my mind.

After the service I did not attend the wake, but returned home, where I got my computer out and started writing. It was only after I had completed the finished version that it dawned on me what an appropriate time and place Spirit had chosen in order to instigate the following poem.

39
A STAR FALLS FROM THE SKIES

It is said a new life will occur,
Every time somebody dies.
And as their souls rise Heaven's way,
A star falls from the skies.

Bringing forth all new beginnings,
Creating life with each new birth.
So those rising souls can take the place,
Of each new soul God brings to Earth.

And although it is just a lovely myth,
Stars do not need to fall.
For God's Summer Land is infinite.
And there is room enough for all.

Yet, what a lovely myth it is.
One spirit climbs, another comes down,
To pass each other in the veil.
One Heaven sent! One Heaven bound!

And for a while a light will dim,
To rest in peace, so goes the story.
Then to awaken from their healing sleep,
To rise again, in all their glory!

Richard John Scarr

40
NAUTICAL TALE

Most of the spiritual poems I write are of a tutorial or informative nature. But on the odd occasion I get something that has me wondering why, as with one particular poem: 'When The Last Hand Comes Aboard'.

I served in the army, and what I know about the navy and ships can be written on the back of a postage stamp. Yet here I was writing about eight bells and dog watches, which meant nothing to me. I even had to go online to see what these phrases meant, and to find out what it was I had written about. But nevertheless, when finished, I placed the poem on the web.

On the following Thursday I was again at Alan's home for healing, and as he too enjoyed spiritual poems, I usually took him a copy of anything I had written. On this particular occasion I took him a copy of 'When The Last Hand Comes Aboard' and I remarked that it was a mystery as to why I had been given this poem, because I knew absolutely nothing about the senior service. But after reading it, Alan shook his head in a kind of wonder, and then he said, "Well, I think I know why!" or words to that effect.

He then went on to explain that the previous evening he had spent half an hour or so speaking on the phone to a lady who had just lost her husband, who had been a regular sailor. Devastated, the poor woman had spent this time pouring her heart out over the phone to him. He then asked me if I would have any objections if he sent her a copy of the poem I had just given him, of which of course I had none whatsoever.

The upshot of this was that a week or so later I received a phone call from the lady, who had been absolutely over the moon to receive the poem. Although it had arrived too late for her husband's funeral, her family and friends had gathered at the water's edge to perform a sprinkling of the ashes ceremony. While a friend and neighbour read the poem, the lady sprinkled her husband's ashes on the water.

I reproduced the poem in Edwardian script on cardboard, and added an 'In Loving Memory Of' to it, and sent it to the lady. She recently informed me that she still reads and takes comfort from it.

As the weeks and months went by, a number of obituaries began to appear online using this poem. Among them was an American woman sailor who had died of leukaemia, and the poem was read by one of her shipmates at her funeral. Another was for Leonard Nimoy, Mister Spock of the Starship Enterprise, who had recently passed over. Another was for Vice Admiral Andries Putter, who had been chief of the

South African Navy. Also, a niece and nephew took the ferry to France and sprinkled their uncle's ashes overboard while the poem was read and the girl rang eight bells on a triangle. No doubt there are others that never find their way onto the web.

As it turned out, some six months later I was to write yet another poem to an old sailor, and it wasn't long before this one too, 'A Sailor For The Lord' began to appear online in obituaries. But I can't help wondering what the reaction of these navy types would be, if they knew these poems were written by an ex-soldier, who didn't know one end of a ship from the other. But nevertheless, Spirit knew what they were doing when they instigated the following poems.

41
WHEN THE LAST HAND COMES
ABOARD

No more a watch to stand, Old Sailor,
For you are drifting on an ebbing tide.
Eight bells have rung. Last dog watch done,
Now a new berth awaits you on the other side.

Your ship is anchored in God's harbour,
And your shipmates, now of equal rank,
Are mustered on the deck to greet you
And pipe, as you ascend the plank.

Her boilers with full head of steam,
Cargo stowed, and galley stored.
Just waiting to get underway,
When the last hand comes aboard!

Look sharp! That hand is you, Old Sailor.
And you'll be sailing out on heavenly seas.
May the wind be ever at your back,
Fair weather. And God speed!

Richard John Scarr

42
A SAILOR FOR THE LORD

Go down to the sea once more, Old Sailor.
For where else would an old Jack Tar be?
But riding the waves, and tasting the brine,
Out there on God's heavenly seas.

With fine weather assured every voyage,
No storms and no clouds in the sky,
With calm blue waters to sail on,
And at night, bright stars to steer by.

With a fine sturdy ship to sail in,
And revered old shipmates to crew.
With an angel riding the masthead,
And land, now long out of view.

What more could an old matelot wish for?
Than to serve as a tar for the Lord.
So welcome, Old Sailor. Stow your kit down below.
And it's an honour to have you aboard!

Richard John Scarr

43
DISTINGUISHED COMPANY

Another poem I was little unsure about, because it seemed to me anyway, to be somewhat unspiritual, is one called 'No Debt To Pay' and it is about someone losing their life on active service. But by now I knew not to question what I was being given. So I sent it to the website who were using my poems at the time, and yet again I was to be proved wrong in my thinking.

A few months later I went online, and up came a Facebook website heading which stated 'Memorial Service for Captain Richard Leary, of the Princess Patricia's Canadian Light Infantry'. But what intrigued me was the fact that my name was included. So I logged on to the web, and up came a memorial service that had taken place in a Canadian military cemetery, with a piper and a bugler etc. The service was being conducted by an army padre.

The gravestones themselves were of the flat kind, in neat rows, and set into neatly mowed grass. But in the centre of the cemetery, a large memorial stone had been erected, around which family and comrades of Captain Leary were gathered, and there were photographs of both sides of the memorial stone. On one side was engraved an image of the captain with the details of his regiment and how he lost his life, while on the other side were engraved all five verses of my poem 'No Debt To Pay'.

Captain Leary had lost his life while serving his country in Afghanistan in 2008. The memorial stone was erected in 2014 by the Royal Canadian Legion, which is equivalent to the Royal British Legion, to commemorate him, and of course, all Canadians who gave, and give their lives for their country. Some months later, again while online I came across yet another Facebook website. It was just a few weeks after Armistice Day 2015. This one had been placed online by the South African Navy to commemorate the sinking of the SAS President Kruger, which sank in 1982, after being in a collision, and in which sixteen sailors lost their lives. There was a picture of the ship, and below it there were eight poems, seven of which were written by well-known poets. It included names like Mary Elizabeth Frye, Henry Van Dyke and Robert Louis Stevenson. And there, nestled between Henry F. Lyte's poem, 'There Is In The Lone, Lone Sea' and Alfred Lord Tennyson's poem 'Crossing The Bar' was my poem, 'No Debt To Pay', and I felt both honoured and flattered to be in such distinguished company.

But what really shook me somewhat was when I logged on to my Facebook account and found some eighty or so posts from all different parts of the world. Each time I logged on, it was to find the list of posts getting longer and longer. I wondered what on Earth was going on, and then it finally registered with me as to the reason why.

Every time someone used one of my poems on Facebook anywhere in the world, the moment they included 'By Richard John Scarr' it was coming up as a post on my Facebook account. But what really surprised me was to find my poem, 'No Debt To Pay' had been placed on Facebook USA, and below the poem was a film shot of Arlington Military Cemetery, with a marine bugler. The website had been well thought out. The object was to click on the film and the marine bugler played the Last Post while the poem was being read, and below that was a calculator which increased by one every time someone logged on to the poem. Astonishingly, at the time of writing, the count stands at a little over three hundred and thirty-seven thousand! And so Spirit had proved once again, that they had a good reason for giving me that poem.

44
NO DEBT TO PAY

I lie at rest — among the best.
And so, you'll understand my pride.
While fighting for a justly cause,
Among the best — I died.

I gave my all without restraint.
And now — with duty done,
I lie at peace without complaint,
And apologise to none!

For you, I gave all my tomorrows,
I gave my life in Freedom's name.
Though time will heal, and dim all sorrow,
Spare me a thought, now and again.

That's all I ask. No debt is due,
No bargain ever made.
Though Liberty is never cheap,
The price was freely paid.

So take with love, the gift I leave,
And never let it go.
I leave Peace and Freedom in your keeping.
It is the greatest gift I can bestow!

Richard John Scarr

45
A CRIMSON PETAL

I am sure my wife knows every poem I have written, and could recite them too. For she often quotes lines from various poems, although they mean nothing to the medium of course. For instance, on one occasion the medium who was giving me a message asked, "Why is your wife talking about bees kissing white flowers?" and I knew instantly my wife was quoting a line from one of my poems, which actually went, 'To watch honey bees kissing wild flowers!'

There is one poem which my wife continually refers to. The poem tells of an elderly husband who dreamed he had his wife in the Spirit World, and was given a crimson rose petal by an angel as a memento of his visit. It was quite obvious my wife empathised with that poem right from the start, for she immediately began to refer to it, and I have been told several times by a medium, "Your wife wants to give you a crimson rose petal." But then I can quite understand her relating to it. For I could quite easily be the alter ego for the man in the poem. The part fits me like a glove, and I could have written it for myself!

46
I DREAMED I WENT TO HEAVEN

Last night I dreamed I went to Heaven,
And when I reached the golden gates,
An angel took my arm and murmured,
"Come inside, no need to wait."

She led me through, and there before me,
I beheld a wondrous sight.
There lay God's house of many mansions,
His Summer Land of Love and Light!

I had never held a sky so blue,
Nor grass so lush and green.
Or flowers of such vivid hue,
Most of which, I had never seen.

And there among the other blooms,
As though in glorious pose,
Magnificent in its majesty,
Was a single crimson rose.

That rose just took my breath away.
It held a beauty so exquisite!
Then the angel plucked a single petal.
"A memento of your visit."

Around me people smiled and waved.
Such a welcoming sight to see.
Some came and shook me by the hand,
As though they had been expecting me.

Then from behind, two gentle hands,
Were placed across my eyes.
Then came a voice I knew so well.
"Guess who, my love? Surprise! Surprise!"

I had never wanted anything
So much in all my life!
And I prayed, "Oh God! Please let it be!"
And when I turned, there stood my darling wife!

We fell into each other's arms,
And tears of joy began to flow.
We kissed and hugged, and cuddled tight.
Each afraid to let the other go.

Then suddenly I realised,
We were young again and in our prime.
Exactly as we used to be.
We had travelled back in time!

Then from all around us others came,
Who had also travelled through.
All the loved ones I had lost.
And some, I never even knew.

We danced and sang, and hugged a lot.
But time in Heaven has no worth.
A year! A month! Or a single day!
Can be a lifetime on the Earth.

One moment she was in my arms,
And we were dancing cheek to cheek.
And then, the next thing that I knew,
I was waking from my sleep.

I lay in wretched silence.
I was old again and all alone.
It had all been just a lovely dream,
But now I was back, and on my own.

Fighting back my tears, I rose,
And moved towards the door.
And as I did, a crimson petal,
Fluttered gently to the floor!

Richard John Scarr

47
CHRISTMAS 2015

There was one poem I wrote, and which I really enjoyed. But it was obvious it had not come from the usual source on the other side. It was called 'A Postcard From Heaven' and it purported to have come from someone in the Summer Land who was having a whale of a time over there. However, I decided not to place it on the web, because I could see no good reason for doing so, for it appeared to me to have no real spiritual connotations, and was just a light-hearted piece of frivolous nonsense.

Later, a lady, who is a member of my church, phoned me to ask if she could have some of my poems. So I sent her some, in which I included 'A Postcard From Heaven'. That was a just a month or two before Christmas 2015. Then, just a week before Christmas she phoned again, and she said she had shown the poems to a friend who was a male nurse. I believe he was the equivalent of a nursing sister. Anyway, he was seeking my permission to reproduce a number of copies of 'A Postcard From Heaven'. Apparently, he was so taken with it, he wanted to place a copy of the poem on the bed of each patient in his wards at his hospital, on Christmas morning. He felt it was so light-hearted, it would raise their morale — and of course, I said go ahead. Then a week after Christmas the lady phoned again to say the poem had been very well received, and had invoked remarks like, "If that is what it is like when you die, then I wouldn't mind going." So I changed my mind, and I placed the poem on the web.

48
A POSTCARD FROM HEAVEN

Dear everyone. Just a card to say,
I am having a wonderful time.
Don't fret that you can't see me.
I promise, I am doing fine!

I am here with all those family and friends,
Who travelled on ahead.
You wouldn't believe the welcome I got.
So much for being dead!

There was Auntie Flo, and Uncle Fred.
Oh, and lovely cousin Giles.
And we had a right old knees-up.
And people came from miles and miles.

We danced and sang, and drank a drop.
Well, what's a party without beer?
But it was all done in the best of taste.
No one gets Brahms and Liszt up here.

You sometimes murmur "Rest in peace,"
But that's the last thing we all do.
Because we're fit and full of energy.
In fact, we are twice as fit as you.

But the funny thing about it is,
We are not aware of time.
And there is no such thing as old age here.
Everyone is in their prime.

Nor is there any illness,
No woes or aches and pains.
No deficiencies or deficits.
Only progress, yields and gains.

And the weather is just perfection.
There's scented flora of every kind.
And colours so vivid and beautiful.
It simply blows your mind!

So please believe me when I tell you,
For these words are most sincere.
And I mean this in the nicest way.
I wish you too were here!

Richard John Scarr

49
WRITER'S BLOCK

The amount of help which I receive from the other side was demonstrated after I had been online one morning.

Someone was looking for a poem for the funeral of a child, and they were trying to find something new to fit the occasion. So I decided I would write one. I sat down with my computer, and after a couple of hours I had managed just one verse, and nothing else would come. For the first time I was experiencing writer's block, and after some three hours, with still only the one verse, and umpteen lines written and discarded, I gave up. I looked at my grandmother's photo on the wall and I said, "I've hit a mental block. Nothing is coming." For some reason I didn't use the word writer's, I used mental. I don't know why.

That was on a Thursday morning, and that evening I went to my church, and one of the lady committee members asked me if I had written anything recently. I told her of my attempt to write a poem for a child's funeral without success. I also mentioned looking at my grandmother's picture and told her what I had said. Because both of us were on duty, we sat at the back of the church. It was an evening of clairvoyance, and during the evening the medium looked at me, and said, "They are talking on the other side about a mental block!" I, and the lady I was sitting with looked at each other in amazement — though, after all these years, nothing should surprise me when it comes to the workings of Spirit. The medium then went on to say, "But don't worry. The block will be lifted and you will be able to get back to your writing."

When I arrived home that evening, I made a cup of tea and settled down to watch TV, and almost immediately bits of verse began to rattle about in my head. So I got my computer out and in no time I was adding verses to the one I had written earlier. By midnight or just after, I had had six working verses of a poem. The following morning, I continued working on them, and by lunch time I had the finished article, which I then placed online. The result can be read as follows.

50
DARLING CHILD

Darling child, we really miss you,
And we thought you were our own.
For we had no way of knowing,
You had come to us on loan.

And like us, God too adores you.
And he showed you so much love,
For he sacrificed you to us.
And watched, and missed you from above.

Your time with us went all too soon.
But in the short time that we had,
It was so magical, and so much joy.
Just to be your mum and dad.

Though we are left with only memories,
Darling child, they are all of you.
For with you went, not just our love,
But our hearts went with you too.

And now God has you back again,
And in his tender care.
You have brought joy back into his heart,
And that of every angel there.

And knowing we too have your love,
Helps to ease the aching pain.
And I'm sure that when our time is due,
God will share you with us once again.

Richard John Scarr

Then, a short time later I again felt the urge to write. So I sat down with my computer, and this time there was no mental or writer's block, and the words came pretty easily. I knew at once it was another poem for a lost child, and after a few hours I was able to place another one on the web.

51
GOD'S LITTLE ANGEL TOO

We only met just for a moment,
For you barely saw the light of day.
God sent you here, then changed his mind,
And took you back the other way.

But it is so hard not to reason 'Why'
And to accept God's will be done.
For it makes us weep how close we came,
To being your dad and mum.

We think about you all the time.
In fact, that is all we do.
We think about you every night,
And every morning too.

We think of you in silence.
We think of you in prayer.
And sometimes in our grief we cry,
"Oh Lord! It is so unfair!"

Just considering what might have been,
Is more than we can bear.
So why then did God let it be?
That we are here, and you are there.

Yet if we could ask him why he takes,
Little angels just like you,
No doubt he'd say the reason is:
You are his little angel too!

Richard John Scarr

52
FOR A DISGRUNTLED SOLDIER

One poem I wrote, I knew definitely had not come from the usual source. I knew in fact, that someone had taken the opportunity to use me for their own ends. Over the course of a couple of days I got fragments of a working poem, which, when I started to write, turned out to be one about a soldier who had served in the First World War, and had fought at the Battle of the Somme, and that certainly had not come from the people who give me my spiritual poems.

After the First World War, Britain was on its uppers and could not afford a large, post-war armed forces, and so a great many servicemen who had been regulars were discharged back into Civvy Street with no job to go to, and little or no money. There was no dole money, or unemployment benefit, in those days, and thousands found themselves on the breadline and facing starvation. Even worse, many came back minus arms or legs, or had lungs completely ruined, or were blinded after being mustard-gassed. So, they were unable to work even if they could find someone to employ them. All they could do was sell matches and boot laces, or beg in the streets. I have no doubt at all that this poem was instigated by one of those soldiers who felt he had been treated shabbily by the government of the time. It seems he is still smarting. So I hope he feels I at least have done my best for him.

I wrote this poem in the spring of 2016, and at the time of writing, I had absolutely no idea the first of July of that same year would be the hundredth anniversary of the Battle of the Somme. But quite obviously, the person who instigated the poem did know it!

53
GOOD OLD TOMMY ATKINS

His uniform was threadbare,
He had his kitbag at his side.
He stood looking at the gates of Heaven,
And wondering if, he would be denied,

He said, "I am not sure I should be here, Lord,
After so much war and strife.
As you know, I was a soldier.
For more than ten years of my life."

"And I know at times, I have been the cause
Of suffering and pain.
And sometimes too, I had to do
What went against the grain."

"But a soldier is a soldier.
And his is not to reason why.
He has no say. And must obey.
He takes an oath to do or die."

"I fought the war to end all wars.
And after I'd survived the Somme,
I was praised and patted on the back.
And thanked by all for being strong."

"It was: 'Good old Tommy Atkins.
You have saved the day'! they said.
'And thanks to you, and your courage too,
We can all sleep soundly in our beds'!"

"But what a different story, Lord,
Once we had won the day.
And normality was back in place.
And all the fear had flown away."

"Then it was: 'Get lost, Tommy Atkins!
The country can't afford your pay.
And so we will have to let you go'.
And they sent me on my way."

"And I found myself without a job,
The pavement for a bed.
Stripped of pride and dignity,
And forced to beg for bread."

"Shivering in shop doorways,
With only hunger for a friend.
My reward for deeds that won the day,
Is so hard to comprehend!"

"And now at last, I am standing here,
Not sure where I should be.
But whatever you decide on, Lord,
Will be all right with me."

Then a gentle voice said, "Tommy, lad —
We have been expecting you.
Come inside, Old Soldier.
And bring your kitbag too."

Richard John Scarr

54
GRANDAD

However, the following poem, I have no explanation for. I never knew my grandparents, apart from my paternal grandmother, whom I only saw a couple of times when I was a young child, and she died when I was little more than seven or eight years of age. So the poem below was certainly not meant for me. Who it was meant for, I simply have no idea?

But I placed it on the web, and I have no doubt it found its way to whoever it was intended for. Although I cannot resonate with it myself, every time I read it, it gets to me, and brings a lump to my throat.

GRANDAD

He was just my dear old Grandad.
Thin on top, and wrinkled brow.
But boy! When he got going,
Could my Grandad spin a tale!

He would tell of wartime epics,
That he'd embarked upon.
Which I listened to with sceptic ear,
Knowing Gramps was stringing me along!

He would tell of trips behind the lines,
Of dangerous deeds well done!
Of coming face to face with foe,
And of battles fought and won!

And I would say to Grandma, "Grandad's tales,
Are growing by the mile!"
But Gran would merely look at me,
Then give a knowing smile.

But I remember thinking at the time,
Though Grandad's tales were just white lies,
And merely told with tongue in cheek,
He was still a hero in my eyes!

Then came the news I'd come to dread.
It simply said: 'Your Grandad's dead!'
That dear old man had passed away,
And a piece of me too, died that day.

Gone were the days when my old Gramps
Would bend my ear, and swing the lamp!
But I was sure the Grandad that I knew,
Would swing that lamp in Heaven too!

No doubt the angels gather round,
As tales of Grandad's deeds abound.
But I bet they take him down a peg,
With, "Come on! Pull the other leg!"

Then one day, Gran came to stay.
And she handed me a small brown case.
She said, "Grandad wanted you to have them.
He knew, with you, they would be well placed!"

When I looked inside, I swelled with pride!
There were campaign medals. Medals galore!
And many of them said: 'For Valour'.
She said, "Grandad won them in the war."

And as the tears rolled down my cheeks,
Gran said, "Your Grandad knew.
You thought he was shooting you a line.
But every tale he told was true!"

Richard John Scarr

55
A GIFT FOR ANNE

I think one of the most touching, and yet mystifying incidents happened again in 2015. That year seemed to be one for quite a number of happenings. Again, it was just a week before Christmas, and I had just finished a poem called 'Then A Nightingale Began to Sing', and I thought that it was a funny time of the year to be writing about nightingales, for they migrate very early in order to escape the winter. They fly off to Africa in July.

The day after I had finished the poem, I received a phone call from a friend and colleague named Anne. Anne is a member of our committee, and is the receptionist at our healing clinic. She is also a devout absent healer, and is recognised as such on the other side. Like me, she lives alone, having lost her husband, Phillip, some years ago; the rest of her family are married and living away. During the conversation she asked me if I had written anything new, and I told her I had just finished a poem called 'A Nightingale Began to Sing' and I asked her if she would like me to read it to her, to which she said yes.

I read the poem to her, which was received in silence.

I thought I heard her sobbing. Then she told me that for the last two nights a nightingale had been singing outside at the back of her house. She said it was so startling and beautiful, she went out into the garden to listen, and she actually asked, "Did you send that bird, Phillip?"

Now as I stated, this was just a week before Christmas. Yet here was a bird singing its heart out on bitterly cold December nights. My first thoughts were that it had to be a bird that sings in winter, because nightingales are long gone by then.

After I had put the phone down, I went online to see if there were any songbirds that sang on winter's nights. As I said earlier, the nightingale migrates early, and only sings at dawn anyway. So I felt it could not be that. The nightjar also migrates in August and September, and also only sings at dawn. But the bird in question had been singing late at night, and the only other bird that seemed to be around at that time of the year was the robin; the male bird again chirps at dawn. But hardly a nightingale!

The following morning Anne phoned me again to say the bird had been back the previous night, singing its heart out yet again, and she was now convinced the poem I had just finished was written for her, and that the bird and the poem were arranged by her husband as a Christmas present for her. I could find no fault with this assumption. It all seemed to fit.

That third night was the last time the bird returned. But shortly after Christmas Anne and I were sitting together in the church, and the medium who was working on the platform at the time came to Anne, and she had Anne's husband, Phillip, coming through. I can't remember his exact words, but he started to talk about the little bird singing outside the house, which verified the conclusion that we had come to. But if there had been any doubts left in my mind, then my wife came through to dispel them.

On the Thursday I was again at Alan's home for healing, and as he laid his hands on my shoulders, he said, "I have your wife, Bell here. And she said to tell you, she knows all about the nightingale, because she had a hand in it!"

By virtue of the fact that Anne and I are friends and colleagues, Bell and Phillip will also be friends on the other side. I am sure they are with us at the Church and in the car when traveling to and from the church. I am quite certain it was Bell who got me to write that poem, and I am sure too, that it was Phillip who arranged for the nightingale to sing outside the house.

How else could a little songbird come to be singing outside on bitter winter's nights, and yet be unaffected by the cold? And with Phillip's help, I have no doubt it also came from the other side. Now I am wondering too, if any of Anne's neighbours heard the bird, or whether it was arranged for Anne's ears only.

Although the poem is now on the web, it was without a doubt written for Anne, for Christmas — and the following is her Christmas present.

56
THEN A NIGHTINGALE BEGAN TO SING

Sleep once more eluded me,
My thoughts again with you.
I know of course, there is no death.
And you have merely made your journey through.

I thought I had prepared myself,
When they told me time was short.
And though I know our parting will be brief,
Still, your going left me so distraught.

Nor has it stopped me missing you,
Or stopped me shedding tears.
It broke my heart when you moved on.
We'd been side by side for years.

Time and time I tell myself,
You are just a thought away.
And although I cannot see you,
You still share my life each day.

And so once again, I faced the pain,
Another sleepless night would bring.
Then in the silence of that midnight hour,
A nightingale began to sing!

The whistling of that little bird.
On a rooftop in the pale moonlight,
Sent a lilting, haunting melody,
Echoing out into the night.

And as I listened to each changing note,
That rose and fell, I knew.
That bird was singing just for me.
A love song, sent by you!

And then I felt your presence,
A gentle touch upon my face.
And as that song flowed over me,
I swear I lay in your embrace.

Then, the warbling of that little bird,
Ceased, as though on cue.
Then with one final chirp! It flew away.
And with it went my sorrow too.

Richard John Scarr

57
FOOTPRINTS

One of the most puzzling poems I wrote actually concerned a work that was not mine, but that of someone else.

I was watching TV one afternoon when little bits of verse began taking shape in my mind. So I did what I usually do. I got my computer out and started to write. At first it didn't register, but as I got to the third verse I realised I was drafting a new version of a very famous and popular prayer 'Footprints in the Sand', albeit in verse format.

It was some fifty or sixty years since I had originally read the story. Someone sent me a copy with a Christmas card, and like most people, I was really moved by it. However, having not given it much thought for many years, I had come across a copy only recently.

After spending some time writing, I had converted the story of the man walking on the sands into a seven-verse poem. Although I read it to my friends at the church etc. I did nothing more with it. After all, this was a famous work, and besides, other people had also converted it to a poetic format, so I was hardly doing anything new. So after sharing it with a few friends, my version of it was confined to the shelf with other poems, and other pages that I had put aside for various reasons, and I forgot all about it.

It must have been some six or eight months later, and I woke one morning with this poem, based on 'Footprints In The Sand' running through my mind, and it was there in my brain practically the whole day. I couldn't get rid of it until I settled in for the evening and became engrossed in the TV. However, a couple of mornings later the same thing happened, and I had the poem running through my mind on and off all day. Over the days following, I awoke several more times with it running through my mind. As you might expect, by this time I was not just bored with the thing, but it was grating on my nerves, and I was heartily sick of it.

Then one morning I woke up and I knew what it was all about! When I placed it on the shelf, I had not stopped to think. If that is where the Spirit World had wanted it to finish up, then I would not have been induced to write it in the first place. They had wanted it to be given a second lease of life, and I was supposed to put it out there in a different form, but I had not done so. That is why I was being pestered with it running through my head, so I dug it out, dusted it off and placed it on the web.

I made sure of course, that the credit for the story was placed with whom it is most commonly attributed to. I only took credit for the conversion to verse.

58
'FOOTPRINTS IN THE SAND' IN VERSE

I dreamed I walked on sandy shores,
And I alone was there.
And stretching forth before me,
My life lay stark and bare.

Every aspect of my being,
Was plainly there in sight.
Every good and bad deed.
Every wrong and right.

And there, beside my footprints,
That followed far behind,
A second set ran parallel.
Keeping step with mine.

Those footprints gave me comfort,
As I traced them o'er the sand.
For in spite of my transgressions,
They remained there, close at hand.

Then, grief and sorrow filled my life.
And it seemed I must atone.
For the second footprints disappeared,
And I was left to walk alone.

I said, "Lord — when at my darkest,
Why didn't you remain?
To see me through my sorrow,
And to help me bear my pain?"

"My dearest child!" the Lord replied.
"Put aside your doubts and qualms.
And know, I too shared your heartache.
And bore you close within my arms!"

Story Author: Mary Stevenson (attributed). Converted
to verse by Richard John Scarr

59
CHRISTMAS 2016

During the last half of 2016, my writing fell off dramatically, and I was getting very little indeed. After a couple of months, I began to wonder what had gone wrong, and why I was failing to find inspiration, and I had a little moan about it to the other side. And then one evening my wife came through to say I would be getting a poem for Christmas. But in the meantime, I should enjoy the respite while I could, because I was going to be very busy in the New Year.

Sure enough, some three weeks before Christmas while watching TV one morning, little bits of poem began rattling around in the old dome. So I switched off, got my computer out, and a Christmas poem began to take shape. When I had finally finished and polished it, I placed it on the web. It was titled 'I Will Be There'.

Again, on the Thursday, when I went to Alan's home for healing, I took him a copy. When he read it, he shook his head, and said, "Amazingly, I know exactly who this is meant for!" and he went on to explain that on the previous day he had given healing to a woman who had lost her husband some years before. As a result, she and her family had not celebrated Christmas since. However, they had decided that this Christmas was going to be different, and they would celebrate it. He then asked if he could photocopy the poem and give it to the woman's daughter who was due to come for healing the following day, which of course I was quite happy with.

The following day the daughter came for healing and he gave her a copy of the poem, and a few days later he received a phone call from the mother to thank him. She told him the poem had been passed around the family, and although it had caused a few tears to be shed, they were all convinced the poem had been meant for them.

Exactly as my wife had predicted, in the New Year of 2017 I began to write these pages, and they have kept me busy ever since.

60
I WILL BE THERE

Hang the fairy lights and mistletoe,
And decorate the tree.
Leave mince pies out for Santa,
And my slippers out for me.

And I'll be there with you at Christmas,
For where else would I be?
But right there in the bosom,
Of my own dear family.

I will be sitting there, in my old chair,
And watching all you do.
And when you sing our favourite songs,
I will sing along with you.

I will be joining in those silly games,
We always used to play.
And hanging onto every word,
That each one has to say.

And when you tell me, "We all love you,"
And toast me, as you do,
Although you will not hear my voice,
I will tell you that "I love you too!"

I will be there with you at Christmas,
As I will be every year.
Until one by one you join me,
For a lovely Christmas here!

Richard John Scarr

61

THE TAKING OF ONE'S OWN LIFE

The taking of one's own life is a very drastic step to say the least, and of course, there are a number of reasons why someone might be driven to doing this. Some people have been known to take their own lives simply to avoid the consequences for some dark deed or deeds they have committed, like murder for instance. However, the taking of their own life in these circumstances will certainly not save them from their day of reckoning on the other side. It will only hasten it.

Other reasons for taking one's own life can range from being grief-stricken, and simply unable to live without someone they have lost, to depression, or to some debilitating and agonising illness from which there is no relief. Another reason of course is mental illness, where the mind simply loses its way.

So then, what happens to those people who, having reached the end of their tether, commit what the Catholics consider to be 'the ultimate sin'? Does damnation await? Does Heaven reject them? Do they go the other way? No! Absolutely not! They, like the rest of us, are met and taken over to the other side and lavished with attention by those taking care of them. And then again by their own loved ones, once they leave the halls of rest. They are doted on even more than those of us who go over in the more orthodox manner. The reason being is that when they awake from their healing sleep, they are guilt-ridden for having taken their own life, and so they judge themselves. But I promise you faithfully, no one else on that side of life judges or holds them to blame, and so everything possible is done to remove that feeling of guilt, and to make them understand they were victims, not offenders. While it might take some longer than others to lose the feeling of guilt, I am sure that eventually, they all come to accept that they were not to blame.

The truth is of course, they could not have killed themselves in the real sense, no matter what they did or how much they tried. It is an impossibility. As I have already stressed, we are literally indestructible. What they do succeed in doing of course, is to kill off their earthly shell, and by so doing, they set in motion their return to the Summer Land. In that sense, they succeed in removing themselves from the environment they find so intolerable.

Nevertheless, because the taking of one's own life is drummed into us from a very early age as being a sin, often the family and friends of someone who has gone over in this way fear for them. Their fear is of course that their loved one will be punished, and maybe denied their place in the Land of Love and Light. I hope therefore that these pages help to put their minds at rest. Their loved ones are in good hands. They arrive safely in the Summer Land, and after being cared for by those wonderful people in the halls of rest, they move into the bosom of all those family and friends who were there to welcome them. And one day, their loved ones on this side of life will be reunited with them too.

The poem dealing with the subject of suicide really came about because one of our church members, a lady named Colette, who was also one of our healers at that time, asked me if I could write a poem on this subject. It seemed she knew a lady who had just lost her son to suicide, and she wanted to pass on to her something that would bring comfort.

I told her that if Spirit had any such poem in mind, then it would make itself known. For she of course knew, the poems I write are Spirit inspired, and I don't write them to order. I then forgot about the matter, but some two weeks later while I was showering one morning, bits of verse started to form. So, when I had finished in the shower, I sat down with my computer and began to write. It became apparent immediately that Colette's request was being granted, and that what I was writing was dealing with the subject of suicide. So I was able to pass onto her a copy of the poem, which she then passed on to the lady who was grieving for her son.

62
BY ONE'S OWN HAND

It is a tragedy at any time,
When a life comes to an end.
But still the sense of loss depends,
On whether family or friend.

But friend or kin, can it be a sin,
When a lost and troubled soul,
Driven by torment too much to bear,
Is no longer in control?

Yet there are those who would condemn,
And cry, "They broke God's law!"
And claim that Heaven will be denied,
To those not deserving any more.

But do they, who set themselves to judge,
And preach, "For them, damnation waits!"
Know so little of their God—
They see him guarding Heaven's gates?

Filled with wrath, and venting spleen!
On such poor souls, whose only sin,
A tormented mind that lost its way,
And could not face another day.

Or those whose every painful hour,
A living hell beyond belief!
And returning home once more to God,
Their only way to find relief.

'Tis enough these souls will judge themselves.
They will not be judged, or held to blame,
But welcomed into Heaven's realms,
And with love, nursed back to health again!

So if you have lost someone you love,
Who went by their own hand,
Be assured they live with peace of mind,
In God's loving and forgiving land.

Richard John Scarr

63
CRYOGENICALLY FROZEN

In the case of having one's body frozen after death, it might be as well to ask ourselves — if we are two beings, then what would be the point of having our physical body cryogenically frozen once we die, in the hope of being brought back to life if a cure was found for whatever brought about our death?

This of course, is a very contentious question, and was triggered because at the time of writing there is a lot of controversy centred around a fourteen-year-old girl who has recently won the right in the British High Courts to have her body frozen, in the hope that she might be resuscitated at a later date, if and when a cure can be found. I sympathise with the fears of her father, that she might be resuscitated sometime in the distant future to find herself all alone in the world. But he need have no fear of that situation arising.

For even if in fifty, or two thousand and fifty years from now a cure was to be found for what took that girl over, all the medical knowledge, and all the skill and cures in the whole wide world would not make one iota of difference! That frozen earthly physical frame would still be without its source of life — its spirit

261

being! So, it could not be resuscitated! For once the spirit discards its physical frame, then that frame cannot survive. It dies! And bear in mind, the physical frame is only created so as to play host to the spirit while it is on this Earth Plane.

So then, even if a cure was to eventually be found, in order to bring that body back to life, the spirit being would have to return from the Spirit World and re-enter its physical frame. And let us not forget; when we go over, it is because it is our time — the time that was allotted to us before we even left the Spirit World. So we must not allow ourselves to become confused by the fact that, when someone has an out-of-body experience because something has gone wrong, and they pass over prematurely as sometimes happens on operating tables, and they are then resuscitated, their passing, even for a few minutes, was not meant to be and so they are sent back because it is not yet their time to make their transition. For if it were, then they could not have been resuscitated!

Just to draw a line under this subject — even if it were possible for our spirit to return to its physical frame months or years later, once the person who took the decision to have his or her body frozen awakens in the Summer Land, they will realise what a sheer waste of time it was, going to all that trouble, because they are not only still very much alive, but in the best of health to boot! And then, even if it were possible to have an eviction notice served on them because a cure

262

had been found back on the Earth Plane, they would almost certainly say, "No way! I'm staying where I am!"

64
IF YOU BELIEVE

If you believe in God the Father,
And if you believe his son,
Was crucified upon a cross,
To cleanse the sins of everyone.

If you believe each one of us
Was placed upon this Earth,
To learn the things that must be learned,
And in so doing, prove our worth!

If you believe a guardian angel
Is watching over you,
Guiding and protecting,
In everything you do.

If you believe we leave this world,
To return from whence we came,
And move once more from life, to life,
To join with loved ones on the other plane.

Then shed no tears when loved ones leave.
For there is no cause for grief.
We are destined all, to meet again,
And the parting will be brief.

So have no doubts, but place your trust,
In all that you perceive.
For it's a far, far better place we meet.
Than that, from which we leave!

Richard John Scarr

65
BREAKING THE BOND

I don't think these pages would be complete if I did not give a mention to the act of breaking the bond that exists between a man and wife, after one of them has made their transition. When a spouse moves over to the Summer Land, the bond that existed between them and the one left behind on the Earth Plane remains intact. It is not severed simply because one has moved to the other side — and when the other spouse moves over, they are reunited and pick up where they left off, but of course, this time as a young couple again.

However, all too often loneliness drives the one left behind to seek companionship with somebody else. It does not necessarily mean they have fallen out of love with their partner in Spirit. But loneliness is a terrible thing, especially where the elderly are concerned. If you are young enough to make a new life for yourself that is one thing. But when you are in the twilight of your years and have been left lonely, that is a different situation altogether, and often elderly people end up forming a relationship and remarrying someone in similar circumstances purely for companionship.

No doubt in many cases the new marriage is meant to be one of convenience, and it was never the intention of the one who remarries to break permanently with their partner in Spirit, and so it is meant to be just a temporary situation until they themselves make their own transition, and can be reunited with the one on the other side. But of course, they are now ex-partners. For they and the one in Spirit are no longer man and wife, because the bond was broken when the one left behind remarried.

The fact is, of course, it would be far better if the one left behind on the Earth Plane merely formed a relationship with their new partner, leaving the bond with their spouse in Spirit intact.

Equally, in many cases the one left behind is reluctant to take up with someone else simply out of a sense of guilt. They feel that if they did so, it would be a betrayal of their loved one in the Spirit World. But I can assure you, if we do form a relationship with someone new, our spouse in Spirit will not be spitting nails and beside themselves with jealousy. Quite the opposite.

Once in the Spirit World, people take on a totally different perception when it comes to their loved ones here on the Earth Plane, and jealousy is no longer a part of their makeup, if it ever was. They spend a great deal of time with us, and know exactly how we are feeling, and the very last thing they want is for their loved one to be lonely. They will actually be grateful to the person we are keeping company with for ensuring that we are not lonely, with the bond still in place, and knowing that when the time comes, they will be reunited with the partner they have left behind on the Earth Plane. They are quite happy with the situation, and fortunately too, where the bond has been broken, there is nothing to prevent us re-bonding by remarrying in the Summer Land.

66
FROM ANNE TO ALAN

The following poem was given to me for my friend and fellow healer, Alan Pilgrim, who is also a widower. Anne, his wife, is often present with my wife, Berenice, when Alan gives me healing. Anne made her transition to the Spirit World quite suddenly and unexpectedly in January 2000, having suffered a haemorrhage.

I had not been to Alan for healing for two or three weeks, because he had been quite ill. And, unbeknown to me, he was really down in the doldrums. Apart from feeling unwell, he had also sent his thoughts out to Anne, asking why she had not been through to him for what appeared to be to him anyway, quite some time. He was really at a low ebb.

As I mentioned earlier, I had not received a poem from the other side for quite some time. But then, quite suddenly I had the urge to write. So I sat down at my computer, and gradually a working poem began to take shape. While actually writing the working verses, I sensed a woman's energy, and mistakenly thought that was because it was meant for a woman. But if I had only known who it was I was sensing, I would have been quite chuffed!

I went to Alan's home the day after finishing the poem, and took a copy with me, never for one second thinking it was intended for him. But the moment he read it, he went quiet. Then he said, "This is for me! I have absolutely no doubt it is from Anne." It was then I learned how low he had been over the past few weeks, and what he had been going through. But that poem did wonders for him! He had resonated with it completely, for there were phrases in it that he knew could only have come from her, and he was quite elated to have received it. It was like a pick-me-up for him, and as a widower myself, I understood just how uplifting something like this could be. And what is more, he had received that poem within forty-eight hours of asking Anne why she had not been through to him of late. However, the poem itself had been presented as though he, Alan, had written it himself, about Anne. And while at first, I had thought Anne had been responsible for it, on reflection I couldn't imagine her writing about herself in this manner and so I came to the conclusion it had to be someone close to her who had instigated it on her behalf, but in such a way that it appeared to have come from Alan. Although she hadn't said as much, I began to wonder if perhaps Bell had a hand in things again.

A few days later I was having a reading with Louise, and was receiving messages from my wife and family, along with those from my two sisters, Vera and Doris. When Louise said, "Alan Pilgrim's wife, Anne, is with them. And she wants to say hello, and to thank you for writing and giving Alan that poem. She said she had been getting quite worried about him, because he had been so ill, which in turn had left him feeling quite low. But that poem was a like tonic for him."

I phoned Alan and told him Anne had been in touch, which pleased him no end, and when I went for healing again later that week, Alan was back looking like his old self again. I told him of my suspicions that perhaps Bell had had a hand in things, and it was then he reminded me that at the time I had given him the poem to read, Bell and Anne had been present. After reading the poem, and at the very moment he had acknowledged the poem was meant for him, he had seen Bell and Anne raise their right arms and perform a high five, as though celebrating success in something, which indicated my suspicions had been correct.

As I took my place in the chair ready for Alan to give me healing, I knew there were a number of my loved ones present, including Bell. As Alan laid his hand on my shoulders, I silently asked her if she had indeed had a hand in presenting that poem to me, and I was immediately rewarded with the cobwebs on my face, and at the same moment I heard her say, "Yes, darling!"

When Alan had finished giving me healing, and as he sat down, I told him of Bell's acknowledgement. He smiled and said, "Yes, I know!"

He then told me that, as he laid his hand on my shoulders, he had become aware of Bell standing beside me. On impulse, he had thanked her for the poem, which she again acknowledged by replying, "You are most welcome!"

Although the poem was personal to Alan, I feel sure he won't mind sharing it.

67
ONCE, UPON ANOTHER LIFE

Once, upon another life, when I had you in my world,
My days would all begin, and end with you.
Day by day, the sun and moon would rise within your
eyes,
Adding sparkle to the stars that shone there too.

I used to say, my guardian angel had cast a spell on
you,
And charmed you so you saw what you should see.
And I sometimes had to pinch myself, just to prove it
true.
You were mine! And you had really chosen me!

You made each day a pleasure. Every minute filled
with joy.
Having you, was everything a spouse could ask.
But nothing is forever. We are here on measured time,
Which sometimes seems to travel all too fast!

One moment we were sharing, once, upon another life.
And then, you were gone, without goodbye!
And as a light went out from my sad and empty world.
A bright new star appeared, up in the sky!

Richard John Scarr

68
ORGAN DONATION

For some people, this is a very touchy subject, and the mere thought of eyes, hearts, kidneys and lungs etc. being removed from their loved ones, after their passing, is just too much to even contemplate. They would baulk at giving their permission for it to happen. Yet, whatever their feelings on the matter might have been whilst on the Earth, their loved ones on the other side would not hesitate for the merest second, and to a man, woman and child would say, "Yes! Go ahead!" For once on the other side they can see the situation from its true perspective.

Once they awaken from their healing sleep to find themselves in a wondrous world, and their spirit body containing every vital organ needed to sustain them in that world, they immediately see the situation they have left behind for what it is.

Apart from their loved ones, all they have left behind on the Earth Plane is a useless piece of flesh and bone that was once their earthly shell, and which they discarded and have no further use for, and of course, will never ever see again. And yet that useless shell contains parts that could give the gift of sight or life to other people who are in need. Parts which are about to be needlessly burned or buried to rot. At that point, if they have not already done so, then they wish passionately they had left behind permission for those parts to be used, and they wish with all their spirit hearts that the person who has the authority to give that permission will do just that!

I promise the reader faithfully; the message being conveyed here did not come from me. But is that of our loved ones living on the other side of life!

69
DAD

Goodnight, Dad. God keep you safe
Until we meet again.
You have left a void no one can fill.
And loving hearts, so full of pain.

Though you weren't one to say it,
We just took your love as read.
For we knew we were your very all.
You always showed what wasn't said!

We never knew a day of want.
You kept us safe in every way.
You nurtured and protected us,
And made us what we are today.

And now we have to come to terms,
And accept that you are gone.
Tomorrow must start without you.
All tomorrows from now on.

Dad, we really miss you.
In oh, so many ways.
And though gone from our tomorrows.
You gave us treasured yesterdays!

Richard John Scarr

70
THE OUIJA BOARD

Without any doubt, one of the most dangerous toys ever devised is the Ouija board. I know for some people, asking '*Is there anybody there*?' appears to be nothing but a harmless game. But it is neither harmless, nor is it a game! Neither will it summon your loved ones to come through from the other side. You will need a medium in order to do that, apart from which your loved ones would not dream of using a Ouija board to pass you a message. For they too know just what a dangerous instrument this board is, and I promise you, they will have nothing to do with it! So please mark these words well!

A medium makes a direct link with your loved ones in the Summer Land. *But a Ouija board links with the paranormal on this side of life!* For there is nothing else out there that this board can link with, other than wandering entities!

So then, when you use a Ouija board, you are literally and deliberately seeking to contact any passing entity, troublesome or otherwise, and inviting it into your home! And some paranormal entities can be quite evil. Sometimes too, they can be very canny.

You can ask time and time again '*Is there anybody there*?' and get no answer. The pointer does not move, and so you think the board hasn't worked. But when things start to go bump in the night, you come to realise it worked only too well! And getting rid of it again can take some doing.

It is also possible you might use the board over and over again with no problems whatsoever. But then you could strike unlucky. For on that one occasion there might be something lurking nearby that will accept your invitation.

Sometimes too, they might masquerade as a child, or even as one of your own loved ones from the Summer Land, in order to gain your confidence; you might link with them again and again with no problems, and so they have you believing that what you are dealing with is friendly and harmless. But eventually they will show themselves in their true colours, and then things will become dark and menacing. It is then you discover you have a problem that you are not able to handle.

There are many recorded instances where people have been plagued with problems simply because they thought a Ouija board was just a bit of harmless fun. In most cases, it takes a priest, or someone who is competent enough to deal with the matter, in order to exorcise the unwanted guest. So if you own one of these boards, do yourself a big favour and burn it! Don't put it out for trash for someone else to find on the local tip. Burn it! That way you could be saving yourself, and anyone else whose hands it might fall into, a lot of frightening problems.

71
FROM SPIRIT TO ME

Some four or five years ago, while sitting among the congregation during an evening of clairvoyance, the medium came to me and asked, "Have you recently finished a poem?" and I told her that I had finished one just two days before. She then said, "They are saying on the other side, that poem was meant for you!" She then went on, "They are talking about someone who passed with bone cancer. And they are saying that you should read the poem again. Because it was meant for you!"

In 2007, just some two years after losing my last stepson, my elder sister, Vera, had passed very painfully with bone cancer. Although she has been through to me on number of occasions since (sometimes accompanied by my wife, for they are very close on the other side), she has never made any reference to her painful passing. Although I was not aware of it at the time of writing, it appears that I had in fact written of her passing, and I can think of no better way to end these pages than to emphasise, with this poem, that when leaving this plane behind, we merely move from life to life! But before I do, I would like to reiterate something I said at the beginning of this book.

Nuclear explosions included — there is not a power or device on this Earth that can destroy you! My friends, you! The real you! The spirit you — is indestructible! And I can't think of anything else on this Earth of which this can be said.

72
MY JOURNEY INTO HEAVEN

It was in those final moments,
With my body racked with pain
I prayed for death to take me,
And yet fearful, just the same.

And then, as though in answer,
The room was filled with light.
I felt two loving arms enfold me,
And my fears were put to flight.

For it was in those final moments,
God had whispered in my ear,
"You are merely coming home, my child.
And there is nothing you need fear."

And so, at peace within myself,
Having lost the fear of death,
I drifted into gentle sleep,
And then, took my last breath.

And when I found myself in flight,
I still felt no alarm.
For to my surprise, I realised,
I was cradled in my Mother's arms.

Though Mum and Dad passed years ago,
And we had mourned their passing too,
I was snuggled in my mother's arms
And was being carried through.

She brought me safely through the veil,
And took me to the halls of rest,
Where I was laid upon a couch,
And treated like an honoured guest.

And all around me others lay,
Who had also crossed 'The Great Divide',
And like me, all filled with silent awe,
To find they too, were still alive.

Then a gentle lady took my hand,
Saying, "Time to heal, my dear.
You are safe and in the Summer Land.
There is no danger here."

"So close your eyes and go to sleep.
Then our Lord can heal your pain.
And when you wake, all will be well,
And you will never hurt again!"

So with a calm I had never known,
I let myself succumb.
And drifted into healing sleep,
So the Lord and I could be as one.

But oh, the joy when I awoke,
And found my parents at my side!
And all the loved ones I had lost,
Were also there. They had not died!

Then, through joy and jubilation,
I again heard God's voice whispering.
"Welcome home my child, to love and light.
There is no death! Nor any sting!"

Richard John Scarr

THE END

73
ENDNOTE

The writing relating to successes covered in the chapters on healing and absent healing, came as an amendment. Apart from my own recovery from asbestosis, I had not previously included anything on successes when I first wrote those pages. But sometime after finishing the manuscript, and while watching TV, I suddenly felt the urge to refer to these sections. Louise had in fact told me a week or so previously that I had an amendment coming, and had even given me the page number 78 of the manuscript. And now, when I turned to this page, it was to discover page 78 was the last page on healing and absent healing. I read the page over, and as I reached the bottom, I knew there was an amendment pending. Then, some of the successes I had witnessed over the years began to occupy my thoughts, and I knew I was about to include some of them.

In a chapter that followed, I wrote of Veronica and of her recovery from bladder cancer, and I also mention that I never saw her again after moving back to my own church. But I knew she was still going strong some four or five years later.

Shortly after I had updated the manuscript with this amendment, I received a phone call from a friend, a lady who is also a quite a good medium, and who sometimes passes on messages to me from the other side. She asked, "Who is Veronica?" which rather took me aback, in view of the fact I had just finished writing about her. I told my friend it was a lady I had given healing to some nine or ten years previously, and that I had recently included her in a chapter in the manuscript I had been working on. My friend said, "She has just come through to me with a lot of gratitude and affection for you."

And so, it appears Veronica too has made her transition.

Whether she was responsible for that amendment, I simply have no idea.

AFTERWORD

My father, Richard John Scarr, passed away in the early hours of Sunday 18th April 2021, aged 90. His suffering was short — just three days — which, if you have read this far, you will know would indicate that his Spirit had led a good life during this particular visit to the Earth plane.

Were he still here now, he would be likely to say that his demise was a timely one, because this book, on which he had spent many years, writing and re-writing, had at last been completed and the contract for its publication agreed. Finally, the world at large would be able to read his insights into the Summer Land and what lies in wait for us once our mortality reaches its end. Therefore, he had finished the work that the Spirit World had asked of him, and his reward for this was a swift return to their plane in order to be reunited with his wife, Berry, and the rest of his family which — as you will have read — meant so much to him.

As I write these words, Dad is at my shoulder. I cannot see him, but as he tells us in his book, he is there, and that knowledge brings comfort to me, as it should to anyone who has lost a loved one.

R K Scarr